GOSSAMURMUR

BOOKS, CHAPBOOKS, AND COLLABORATIONS
BY ANNE WALDMAN

On the Wing

O My Life!

Giant Night

Baby Breakdown

Memorial Day (with Ted Berrigan)

No Hassles

The West Indies Poems

Life Notes: Selected Poems

Self Portrait (with Joe Brainard)

Sun the Blonde Out

Fast Speaking Woman

Journals & Dreams

Shaman/Shamane

Sphinxeries (with Denyse Du Roi)

Polar Ode (with Eileen Myles)

Countries (with Reed Bye)

Cabin

First Baby Poems

Makeup on Empty Space

Invention (with Susan Hall)

Den Mond in Farbe Sehen

Skin Meat Bones

The Romance Thing

Blue Mosque

Tell Me About It: Poems for Painters

Helping the Dreamer: New & Selected Poems, 1966–1988

Her Story (with Elizabeth Murray)

Not a Male Pseudonym

Lokapala

Fait Accompli

Troubairitz

Iovis: All Is Full of Jove

Kill or Cure

Iovis II

Kin (with Susan Rothenberg)

Polemics (with Anselm Hollo & Jack Collom)

Homage to Allen G. (with George ScÿeemanN)

Donna Che Parla Veloce

Young Manhattan (with Bill Berkson)

One Voice in Four Parts (with Richard Tuttle)

Marriage: A Sentence

Au Lit/Holy (with Eleni Sikelianos & Laird Hunt)

Zombie Dawn (with Tom Clark)

Dark Arcana/Afterimage or Glow

In the Room of Never Grieve: New & Selected Poems, 1985–2003

Fleuve Flâneur (with Mary Kite & Dave Kite)

Structure of the World Compared to a Bubble

Outrider

Femme Qui Parle Vite

Red Noir

Nine Nights Meditation (with Donna Dennis)

Martyrdom

Manatee/Humanity

Matriot Acts

The Iovis Trilogy: Colors in the Mechanism of Concealment

Soldatesque/Soldiering (with Noah Saterstrom)

Cry Stall Gaze (with Pat Steir)

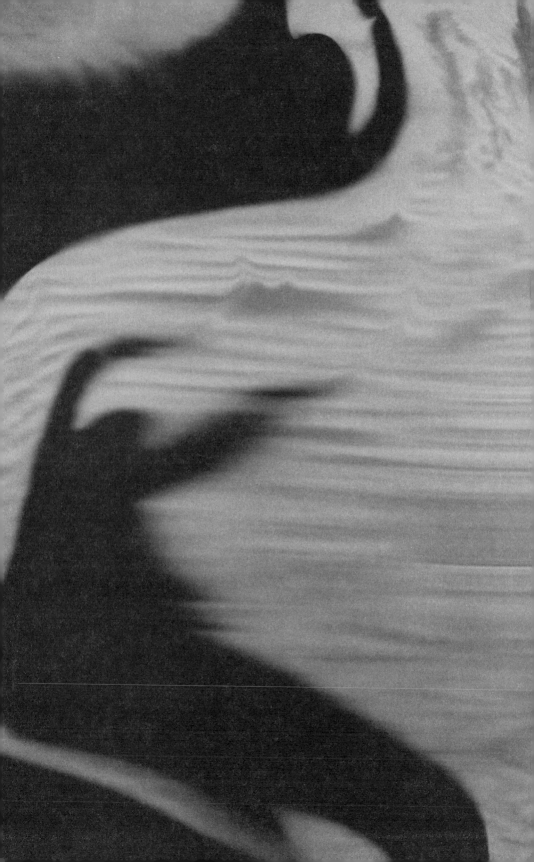

GOSSAMURMUR

Anne Waldman

PENGUIN POETS

PENGUIN BOOKS
Published by the Penguin Group
Penguin Group (USA) Inc., 375 Hudson Street,
New York, New York 10014, USA

USA | Canada | UK | Ireland | Australia | New Zealand | India | South Africa | China
Penguin Books Ltd, Registered Offices: 80 Strand, London WC2R 0RL, England
For more information about the Penguin Group visit penguin.com

First published in Penguin Books 2013

LIBRARY OF CONGRESS CATALOGING-IN-PUBLICATION DATA
Waldman, Anne, 1945-
  Gossamurmur / Anne Waldman.
pages cm
ISBN 978-0-14-312308-8
I. Title.
PS3573.A4215G67 2013
811'.54—dc23   2012040614

Printed in the United States of America
10 9 8 7 6 5 4 3 2 1

Set in Fournier MT Std
Designed by Ginger Legato

what are the limits of the body?

for Akilah Oliver
poet, teacher, catalyst

(1961–2011)

        Nevertheless,
It is dangerous to be named
and makes you mortal.
If you have a name
you can be sold
you can be told
by that name leave, or come
you become, in short
a reference, or if bad luck
is large in your future
you might become an institution
which you will then mistake
for defense. I could
now place you
in a column from which
There is No Escape
and down with The Machine
will always recognize you.
Or a bullet might be Inscribed
or I could build a maze
called a *social investigation*
and drop you in it
your name
into it—

Please! I implored him
you terrify me.
What then, I asked
is my case? looking into
the Odd toed ungulate's eyes
who had his left leg resting on my shoulder.
The mortal can be described
the Gunslinger finished,
That's all mortality is
in fact.

                —*Gunslinger*, Edward Dorn

The valley spirit never dies.

It's called *dark female-enigma,*
and the gateway of dark female-enigma
is called the *root of heaven and earth,*

gossamer so unceasing it seems real.
Use it; it's effortless.

—*Tao Te Ching,* sixth-century BCE translated by David Hinton

ACKNOWLEDGMENTS

With gratitude to Peter Warshall, MaelstrÖm reEvolution, the Tamaas foundation, *Conjunctions*, *Denver Quarterly*, *The Brooklyn Rail*, Bhanu Kapil, Ambrose Bye, Pat Steir, Alexis Myre, Elliot Colla, Sawko Nakayasu, David Gitlen, Apsara DiQuinzio, and Gina Maher, who in her generosity gave home and shelter to this writing. Making up a small portion of the work are lines from *Entanglement* (2009) and *The Value of Small Skeletons* (2011), movies by Ed Bowes and several pages appear in *The Air We Breathe: Artists and Poets Reflect on Marriage Equality*. Also, sincere gratitude to my editor, Paul Slovak, who has supported my poetry for many years.

GOSSAMURMUR

Gossamer is not used by any branch of biology
but there are phenomena soft, sheer, and gauzy
light and flimsy
delicate, tenuous, and airy
Gossamer means *summer goose*
The time the goose plucks winter down
and lines her nest
        and the down caught
  in the tundra sun and breeze
sails off glistening
In Sanskrit: *ghans-sem*

Probably a time some humans
collected either the goose or

down for themselves

For other species, gossamer is always transient
turns more tensile
pliant
or rigid

That's the fabric of inner bones and muscles
and arteries

Moth cocoons, caddis fly catch-nets

Woven with a protein called collagen

The gossamer bodies of plants—
dandelion fluff or cotton—
are of cellulose

Cellulose is a complex sugar

A way pliancy can supplant stiffness

The way tensile strength prevents fractures

Some gossamers have extension

(distance divided by original length)

And the questions

stretch until you break

stretch until you cannot snap back

stretch until you reach some threshold of safety?

Poem as lute string.

       plot rescues sanity.

recuses identity its floating world. . . .

       and allegory tests calamity

resilient or under siege

Once how delicate the gauze that adheres to and flicks off identity. Flips it. Becoming cartography. *Gossamurmur* occasions a transgressive vein, a body poetics with a bifurcated protagonist indicating two simultaneous and alternating realities. Often alarming. She and She. By way of a mundane *duplicada* experience (I noticed her she had a funny dayglow wig on she said my name when asked hers) I discovered my credit union had another client with my exact name. At one point our accounts had become transposed. I thought of Borges and his "doubles" and Thomas Mann's *The Transposed Heads*. I fantasized about this meticulous, oddly coifed other and how she might spend *my* money. And then how I might spend *hers*. Bodies in a *materia infinitum* world that levels down to charnel ground. Where all detritus grinds down. Sing you there, my *duplicada*. I will find you there. We will spend our phantom money. We will meet without name without body without debt but that of past action in nominative karma. Who did what to whom. I will be your other, wisp of consciousness . . . and you will be mine in token of our name, a rare coinage.

And she was the trigger, the apparatus, of my composite allegorical destruction or rather of all I cared about in the mundane world which was the survival and oral archive of an excellent poetry and record of a temporary autonomous zone from which it emanated, close to a high-altitude Divide. And she was a grand *infinitum*, a robotic tool of the fits and starts of the dread Deciders who in a trajectory of willful ignorance and anti-art psychosis wrought their weird embryonic magic on my person and psyche and the fragile cassette and song files of a fleeting transitory poetics. . . .

I spent her account on medicinal herbs and lozenges. Items for longevity. I spent her dollars on salvation, on books of remorse and redemption, on a complete revelatory encyclopedia, on the health of another, on a ticket to the opera—it was Wagner, it was *Parsifal*, it was on a night of full moon, he held me, and we wept. *I hate it! he said. I hate this spectral life! I wish it would all disappear!* I said, *I love it!* And I donated to numerous causes including those toward the well-being and salvation of many endangered species. Whose sounds and cries and metabolic thrum and hum might soon be silenced. . . .

The Sulawesi Dwarf Kingfisher, Ultramarine Lorikeet, Stump-Tailed Macaque, Sulu Bleeding-Heart, Tristan Albatross, Tehuantepec Jackrabbit, Zoe Waterfall Damsel, Zingis Radiolata, Zhou's Box Turtle, Yellow-Blotched Palm Pit Viper, Yellow-Breasted Bird of Paradise, Mozart's Frog, Old Narwhal, Marbled Malachite, Lesser Dwarf Lemur, Patzcuaro Stream Frog, Moluccan Cuckoo, Wild Asian Buffalo, Hyacinth Macaw, Hyaline Fish, Holy-Mountain Salamander, Pearly Parakeet, Javan Shrew-like Mouse, Ozark Cave Arthropod, Fiji Crested Iguana, Mexican Blindcat, Firethroat, Little Spotted Kiwi, Dwarf Tinamou, Esmeraldas Woodstar, Cuban Crocodile, Cordelia's Crow, Chinese Pangolin, Dalhousie Hardyhead, D'Abrera's Tiger . . .

I gave her money to organizations aiding the lives of plants, and of innocent victims beset by the tragedy of the New Weathers. Tornados occurring here and there should not be occurring there and here. Surprise of tsunami, shock of hurricane, earthquake, and fires prone to these extreme drought zones. I bought hashish and other elixirs. I spent carefully, I spent wisely, I spent with a sense of grace. I traveled to a jungle and washed my world away with a bitter vine. I had anthropomorphic visions. I saw demons with metal mandible parts, I saw impostors everywhere that resembled the people I knew, but if you look more closely at her ring, that is not *her* gold ring; it is not a gold snake ring with ruby eyes . . . look more loosely at the stone around her neck; that is not *her* onyx, her face suddenly unglued, askew . . . that is not *her* eyebrow. I saw myself transformed and disembodied and disentangled, then reconstituted. I heard voices. I invented a new name for my publishing company: *Sayonara*. I was confused.

She spent my hard-earned working-cash on dining out. Taunting me as if to say, *You are poorer than you will ever be.* That was it. She raised the ante on dining out. She was a classic, addictive carnivore.

We crashed. Or rather she crashed.

I kept writing checks on our twinned account. I spent hers on salvos. On political campaigns. On candidates that furthered the existence of literature. On death and a birthday. I spent hers on an exit strategy that almost worked. I died a little. A part of my identity chipped away. I did not mind and then I did.

What are we worth? I mused. *What is our exchange value on this vast meddling market?*

I left my marriage. I left multiple lovers. I abandoned the rock star I had served day and night. I walked home late and thought again of our finite coinage, our value as a minted "thing." I saw she-who-carried-my-name on Patchin Place. Not far from the credit union near where I lived. There was a moon hung low in the sky. I encountered the djinni of Djuna Barnes whom I had seen frequently in this place decades before, aging. . . . Djuna had morphed. She had crashed. She was restricted in her motion.

Her eyes had the glow of smoldering cinders.

The double is always present in our psyches. I follow her. What is hidden responding to what is revealed is the binary axis on which the investigation pivots. I hide behind the screen of my own investigation. Still longing for my shadowy, more flagrant, more casual other *cause*. The double writes books on desire and the need to colonize the host bodies of the Deciders.

Long fascinated by the stories of "double women," I pick up the tale of the two Lilas, which presents us with the woman's view, and that of a double or shadow. In one story the woman has two husbands—a demonic husband whom she loathes and an incestuous lover whom she adores. Both women share a single lover in the other story. He is cunning. In older variants of the tale of the shadow woman, the shadow "other" serves to protect the woman from any defilement or stain at the hands of the demonic husband. The shadow also keeps the "pure" woman of the real world separate from the lustful, passionate woman of the subterranean world. The shadow woman seems to be more like a shard of a dream. I study types of dreams described by Cicero in *De Divinatione* lifted from Philo Alexandrinus's *De Somniis*: night apparition, oracular, enigmatic— *horama, oneiros, chrematismos*. There is also a sense of double *universes* as time and space are both mapped separately in a Vedic cosmology, although the two dimensions are parallel. This mythology tells not only of double people at two points on a spectrum, but of double worlds that provide two layers of the spectrum of space-time. The doubles in myths or dream or illusion make possible a process that seems to protect the presenter-in-this-life from the dangers of complete solipsism. *Or you might go mad. . . .*

The Deciders kept interrupting the narration. They controlled the Base.

The Deciders create their factotums; they create Impostors.

What might they do to interrupt progress? They were bound in that—interrupting progress. Was it just a suicidal death wish for all humanity? They were in on the ruse to circumvent the machinations and desires of lovers of language, of linguistic fun and folly, of non sequiturs or where you write a poem without knowing where it would lead, where the poem was like the mind of the poet, stopping and stuttering and starting. Indeterminacy—how language pushes on you, and if the relationship between word and concept is arbitrary, then the attitude toward language must change. Instability of logic, ad hoc forms, delete every second word . . . might . . . do . . . interupt . . . they . . . bound . . . that . . . progress . . . it . . . a . . . death . . . for . . . humanity.

They wished to interfere with the desires of the Original Anne, she who writes this, who struggles in real twenty-first-century agon to warn the world of the impending collapse of generative language, of the Deciders' impulse to control or destroy the narratives that are anything but master. That are anything but fascist. That are anything but gloomy. That are anything but manipulative. They record heart and breath and tongue and pause. And rest in analogues of thinking one thought instanter upon another. And the New Weathers? Take heed of them in our endangered orality.

Spool the tape. Rewind. Digitize. Listen. Good a thousand years?

In many mythologies a sexually or psychologically assaulted woman is permanently transformed into a plant or an animal. Would this transformation preserve the resources of future revelation that she carry this seed underneath her inchoate identity? Circumvent deciding in a human form.

Deciders resent an upstart woman with upstart larynx.

Consider:
Minthe the spearmint
Leuke a white poplar
Side, pomegranate
Lotis, the lotus tree

Daphne, laurel
Philyra, the linden

     Kallisto
Io

See: *Versipellis*
and therianthropy

Notice the ways they morph on you.

The Decider stood hovering over me with menace saying, *"I thank you for your passion, Original Anne."* He was making a list of all the Deciding Categories the Original Anne would be excluded from.

Original Anne looked deep into the eyes of this Decider, I would almost say lovingly, into the eye-pools whose shapes within turned mosaic, congealed to bits of colored glass. . . . She then saw within the finer particles more blocks of menacing form relaxing then realigning to shape and position, to the posture of the troubling things of this world.

A car with recliner, chauffeur, a screen on which played a Decider fantasy of Decider himself, suave and buff at the top of a stair exuding an exquisite control and lauding it over a servant at the bottom bustling along with a tea serving and vial of cognac to fire the drink:

"Up here, you idiot!"

Kagero Nikki (*The Gossamer Years*) is the name of the novelistic diary of a noblewoman in Heian Japan. The diary is in some sense a protest against the marriage system of the woman's time. Conjecture ensues, but *Kagero* might mean "gossamer" in the usual sense, as in "a film of cobwebs floating in air in calm, clear weather" (*Merriam-Webster*) or "the shimmering of the summer sky."

I add this "murmur" to you, suggesting a register of underlying voices, fond reader, perhaps "gossip," sometimes rising to a state of cacophony. In this reality the Heian woman rarely ventured beyond her own veranda; "life moved indoors," the translator notes, and often *to a murmur* . . . But her diary was lush with descriptions of robes and tear-strained sleeves, of lovers' faces and wiles and other accoutrements of a restricted social world.

Will you meditate upon the coolness of floors? Sit by a viewing station and wait, shift in a fold of a summer night dress, folded light, or light plays off the pool's water, koi fish shimmer, and what is ascertained of uncertainty, of delay, glints of aqueous fish light, scales like shiny pennies, dressed-up illusion. Agitation. Tear-stained sleeves. Will you meditate upon a tear-stained sleeve?

I see my own gown here, wet with tears of frustration and longing. What to do in rescue? Night after night, collapsed into tears.

Had no certainty of the days ahead.

Identities true and false, romantic and sexual love, seclusion, the *duplicada,* witchcraft, social and gender hierarchy, divination, as well as a contemplation of the multi-universes "out there," as one gazes into the double helixes of night sky from a restricted vantage point. Entwined, entangled. Two new planets have been named today.

And then I thought *through* doubles, through other names and forms in which I could transcend the earth without moving.

A vow, a promise at the deathbed of a beloved poet, elder to this clan, then assured and commanded me I must be cohesive, that I must be synchronized and strong. I must guard the Archive even at this many-leagues distance, at all costs, under threat of psychic murder and dissolution. I would lock myself in the mind of poetry, in the library within the library of that mind of poetry. Delight in the monastic *Arkheion*, a house, a domicile, an address, residence of the archons, those poets who command . . . and preserve.

She studied allegories and what within those constructs would muster courage. How a small idea may expand to gianthood. How big is imagination the Deciders would never understand. She entered a chthonic castellum, a physic prison, at the instigation of others, those Deciders who would use her to advantage, steal her secrets, and—threatened by her power, her sharp tongue, her stylus—attempt to keep her "inactive," while a simulacrum donned her identity in the phenomenal world. Poetry was a threat in the phenomenal world.

She wrote *I thought through doubles* as a goad to stay rooted, which was, of course, as she attempted, impossible. She was pushed into being *in the in-between*.

Transcend the earth without moving. The fish were on their own sleeves tonight.

The writing itself of this what-you-call-it, of weaving of elongating of investigating of cannibalizing of cherishing of what one might learn from this in doing it this tale became difficult. She once lived on a street named Goss. Or the release she might experience from the doing of it the "it" became harder. We called our poetry "works" back then. You built a work in your mind of architecture. Works in the shapes of mastabas, pyramids, stupas, of protracted wars that required sophisticated artillery, matériel, cybertech designs of infinite and obstructive methodology, works that worked their way into your private psyche, "works" that are sentences and secret rhythms and senseless. Of the music inside singing outside on sleeve of herself. She lacked confidence in the ability of logic to persuade others what was at risk. It was as if she was being drained by circumstances around her metabolism, the project she had worked on more than half a life, a *moisopholon domos*, a house of the muses, a community to house and sustain imagination was in jeopardy. It was a dark castle she inhabited now, surrounded by a forest of negative mind-sets. Eager to extract slices of intelligence, to dumb and numb the wild mind out of the guardians of Archive, wanting to cut up and trash the experience that voices now disembodied existed, haunting voices singing, sighing, imploring you to *listen* your way through consciousness. There had been fires, flames whipping at the edge of her experiment, *an alchemical thaumaturgic linguistic zone*, surrounded and occupied and compromised by the dangers of Deciders and Impostors. There had been floods. Why did they wish to take over and inhabit her Utopia? De-story it. Destroy. Why did they resist and seek to subvert a metabolism that could carry us into the future glorious Archive? When the earth would be so denuded, bereft of idea and poetry. There had been a drought, long in the making, spread now coast to coast. A culture-drought.

Her Double was gaining in power. In a plot that would keep her Ever-the-Original Anne on edge. All eyes went to the new Anne. She had become a household word.

Impostor is also con is consummate concomitant con is cardboard is false convivial, cunning con. She shouted out to whoever was listening, *You know who you are.*

She wrote her message on all the convivial networks. *You know who you are.*

What was in the Archive?

It held a slice of belletristic time, radical and political. It held
multiple discourses on the limits of the body, on unlimited and
de-limited consciousness. It held *Sprechstimme* and performance, and
high talk and *sacre conversatione*. It held a new poetry and beyond

The other Anne stole into the room
She lived on the other side of the wall
The other Anne was a succubus
She bled the true Anne

She wanted to acquire the ideas and stratagem of the Original Anne,
the blueprints for the Utopias and zones Original Anne labored to
create in her frenzied defense of poetry and Archive and prosodiacal
discourse

She wanted to acquire the root conversations of the Original Anne
She wanted to hack into delicate twists of language and torques of
intuition that graced the corridors of the conversations of many of
value to the Original Anne

who spoke in twilight language, who spoke in runes, whose
enigmas of tone and gesture
   were magnetizing

The Impostors wanted to be those many, those voices in the corridor
or they wanted to own them

They abhorred beauty, beauty terrified them, but actually they
wanted the power of beauty

The other Anne wanted to acquire the lovers of the true Anne
and sleep with all the lovers of the Original Anne

The other Anne stole half the things in Anne's world with impunity
She usurped her words, her tone
She usurped her poetry
She wanted to acquire the tissue and neurons of her past lives
She wanted to go back that far
To visit the larynx of the original Anne

And she made extravagant claims for the love of others who had
loved the Original Anne

She mouthed the words of the others who had been mouthing words
for Original Anne

She mouthed philosophy and she spoke of binaries

She mounted the many things that related to Anne she announced,
I am Anne

A school was under siege
Poets held in *aporia*, a space of waiting and stasis
Dead poets whose voices waited to be resuscitated
   whose words were locked up in time, in a dead zone
   needing rescue
   needing care, attention

Original Anne held a small cassette of John Cage in her hand,
magnetic tape fallen off its cheap plastic sprocket
held it as Buddha might the human bone
wondering—if *this*, then *that* . . .
birth, old age, sickness, death. . . .
She took out a bobby pin and scrolled the tape back on its tiny wheel
We will keep this sheltered, and listen

. . . while out in the choppy elemental world the Chacaltaya glacier melted away,

melted away in a repetition,

continuous repetition melting, subsiding

water upon water drop

weather was changing

Respiration came to mind

Breathing with weather or breathing-in-weather had morphed

There were persistent rumors of the demise of predictable weather systems

We had many re-coded names for the origin of whispering

We had—our tight poetry clique had:

Hwisprian
Murmare
Khwis
Wispelen
Hwispalon
Wispeln
Wispern
Hviskra
Hwistlian

We had one another, poets on the altiplano

We played some games near zones of silent mutation near the centers of our own ambition

. . . whistle or beckon, seek . . . hide . . .

The street she said always comes-with-a-poem

We were confident language might be in love with us

We fortify her we said she will not abandon us let us down

She is with us everywhere in the streets and valleys and tundra of her poem

Try to compose in a streetwise way Archive whispered

land is compromised,
rivers are stressed,
beauty still exists in relation of that time
  fresh out of sleep
  and glaciation, a tongue
  finds way in in beauty
                        this is our cause and to notify the others

passersby bid witness here (because we protested always in public space)

DNA's empire economy: "sound the decibels" and bid witness

 as you approach Camino de las Estrellas a place for walking
              under faint stars, bid witness and in the narrow straits
of the medina
where moon awakens, bid witness
            and from my eastern pavilion, moon is like a scimitar

I would dream of Parsifal a woman
play the part of seeker
write a feminized version under metabolic planet and stars

seek the sacred vessel to hold these phones and phonemes
raise the golden dagger to strike out against their abuse

            Holy Grail a blank check for these times

what is your treasure   what remains, Scheherazade?

She was wanting to possess manna
map redividing coalescing
that civilization could get smarter

recidivism, what is it   a chance operation?

Original Anne
had lived and traveled with the grand old poets
with the grand old poet-mouths
she lived in their homes
she ate their food
she ate the vegetables grown from their gardens
in a paradisiacal valley with the scent of cherry blossom

she labored at the desk of elders
in a room with gaslight. . . .
dim restless desk of Archive

mor-mor
Sanskrit *murmurah*

what is it but a crackling fire

syndicates of samsara abuzz

mormyrein = to roar to boil

murmlenti

softly spoken (hidden) words inside the castellum

expression of discontent by grumbling

mordant sound awash everywhere
in collapsed intellect

does a stone giveth sound   doth it rend and break

surpass us, down-low

>>rive<<

what are they saying about originals, artifacts of poem-bodies
that we are too risky in two-faced diplomacy that we go hidden and
in exile?

"poetry a Socialist enterprise!"
"smacks of elitism!"
"who cares?"
"you know what the Poet said
'poetry makes nothing happen'"

risky in liability, that our originality is irksome and dangerous

she is mine or *she* is like me

this is how the world gets at me, "me" says we're equal
    in our micro-world, contentious conglomeration of pronouns
or is *she* taking me over

or in what manner in what bondage is *she*

they decided on this and other important grammatical matters
a kind of lower-case theft:

steal fire

steal salt

steal agenda of one who was struggling inside an organization of art

a words-only school finding new words for "containment"

A very first Decider of the First Rank of Regulation

was striving to ascend a ladder in a workplace like a corporation

a corporation where Deciders wrestle with "packages" and

"redundancy" and "assessment" and various means and methods of

power "relaxment" created so that Deciders may decide

He was privy to a range of lightly inclined enhancement and free-

association infusion practices which help Deciders decide

"library"	:	"closet"
"poetry"	:	"wastebasket"
"rhizome"	:	"in the drawer"
"metabolism"	:	"marketability"
"experimental"	:	"pencil"
"metaphor"	:	"paperweight"
"biosphere"	:	"curtain"
"curtain"	:	"library" and so on. . . .

But the first Decider of the First Rank faltered in a conference call

enraged that he was not getting his way on a crucial decision

about "accessibility" about "partnering" about a once-in-a-lifetime

"merger"

He broke down trembling at the end of a long mahogany conference
table

"Am I not a Decider?" he whimpered into his soft manicured hands

The Tenth-Rank Decider decided to join in, weeping and trembling
a strange symbiosis among Deciders
they could feel one another's frustration and pain

Not having the power to fully decide was a hell realm

They pushed through an agenda with cajolement and duplicity
with corporate advancement
with cynical advantage
closeted rage and hope of ownership and revenge

What is poetry to the robotic-drone dreamworld
rash of noise   hum   nonsense syllables

Talky entertainment boxes you can't control by land or by sea,
in the air in sky that was unconditional once, and vast

A taxi pulls up and you get in, subjected to the squawk box inside,
deadening emblem of end-time in incipient dark age

This is fascism you mutter into your muffler

Take me to the next extreme

storm clouds gather on the horizon

"What's a poetry portal?" the Third-Rank Decider asks, sweating into his uncertainty and possible loss of control

A window onto the whole world. . . . listening back at you

The Deciders took Anne apart organ by organ, sinew by sinew. And they copied these parts into the husk of the new Anne with skill and dark intent. As they did this they would pause, mewling into their sinister Autopsy:

"Little organ of Original Anne, what can you do for us now?"

"Little eyes of Original Anne, what will you accomplish now?"

"And you, sinews that bind operation of motion, where walk you now?"

"Tongue that composed many ballads and odes for your time, how will you sing?"

They gloated in their desire to reveal the nothingness of all things, and to murder poetry.

They could not remove or mutate her consciousness, which stayed intact in the retreat and isolation of the Original Anne.

They made their copy, a mockery of the Original Anne, undoing the manna of Original Anne, who they cast into a virtual prison while they went about their plot of alienating humans from their linguistic natures. Language would become separated, torn from its vital dwelling place. Humans would be living out history and a life of unrelenting State without poetry. The Archive of the multiple voices was endangered, years in the making, to preserve breath and intellect, imagination's other place, as psychic inscription and to let humans of the future know some of us were not just killing one another.

"*You would never guess,*" they said, "*look at our creation, a perfect simulacrum.*" And they looked to a time of acquiescence where the populace would be silenced. Where the attention span of humans, ever-waning, would ride the waves of mediacrats, and hear tell endlessly, monotonously, the slow drip of the undulating fortunes of celebrity worlds and become even more accustomed and inured to the beat and thrum of war.

And more in lockdown. And more and more in lockdown.

There was a Decider of the Fifth Rank of the State of Rectilinear Space as it applies to a subject's metabolism

Decider of how many gold stars on a bonnet

Or for one entering the room of major decision-making feeling diminished, there was a Decider sitting behind a massive desk of protocol and power

Facing windows of gray light in sad anemic offices over which more Deciders preside

Deciders of who leaves or stays, who gets laid off, who must be demoted

Who closes rank

It was not a happy world.

Original Anne mumbled in her prison/castellum:

Yes, you could lose your mind

And in captivity: pray if all else fails

And read all books while you still have privilege
in the library-prison world
Rimbaud you are source on the original list
Everyone abides you
Blake come soon and next and often
Dante Cavalcanti Sappho Hafiz Mallarmé all Saints of Poetry

And Saints also of any holy thing

Our Lady of the Pillar, in mind out of sleep tonight

St. Sephra Seraphim, be with me

Goddess of Scriptures and Scriptoriums hold fast

Simon Magus's death giveth fire

Apostle Peter is watching, nary no scold

St. Francis of Assisi suspended above earth and watching

Christina the Astonishing help my troubled bifurcation

Rebbes, mullahs take heed

Archangela Girlani hold up the 3-brane world

Buddhas of compassion everywhere

Please release us from your spider's cradle

Peaseblossom, Mustardseed O pray appear

Deciders: return to your neutralized stations in the shadow world

Your language stops revealing anything,
instead revealing the nothingness of all things

Can we dream our own melancholia for what is irretrievable?

The Deciders think the troubadours were a problem

Erasure, a suicide pact

Magic doubles deceive you
The stuff of your sex and the projection of mind . . .
This is normal and sinuous
They are taking you apart in the time/space machine

Reading one upon another in fulmination of other lives
Don't go crazy, Original Anne

Let's go excavate some poetry
on papyrus   in cuneiform   magnetic tape

         solid-state memory *save on the cloud*

faced by an electronic pentameter

"claw out some poetry eyes?"

                save on a cloud

switching code in the runnels

circling a moat devised as a first-front defense aporia
   keep moving, keep dancing

mountain shifts

   ice crystals form on her duplicated mouth

   a forked path on forehead
more streaks on screen bank

which way to caress a broken brow

familiar as your deadly Belle Dame sans Merci

reels of orality

chalk, obligatory calcium
      in marrow of women who wrote in ancient diaries
bemoan their Heian imprisonment

shape of crying like a mourner
you could establish in humility this pose

"shape of a mourner"

who are we kidding?

when Deciders cheer inside

break sound they said
manipulate pitch

   vocal cords
phonation's
 a discourse
  for the impostors

what is language?

"We use it, don't we?
in our copious memos, in our 'releases,' in our
power documents
in our homilies to the world
cliché quotations on
life
suffering
the passage of time
on Patriotism
on the need for downsizing
on 'tighten your seat belts'
on finding the childlike naive spirit of servitude within the workplace
don't look now while you are looking away we will replace you
with our own poetry, our mission statements of despair"

This is a template application for the Deciders
images of rows of normative coffee mugs
as if we are having a pleasant chat over
a freshly brewed cup of virtual coffee

Hardest problem in science
  is the origin of language
    "we bend science," they say

prelinguistic system among primates
our early human capacity for song

level of public trust

to sing your song
                             bend or break it

in ritual/speech evolution

100,000 years ago to

Homo ergaster, the first human to vocalize

"can we find her and bend her over?"

"vocal grooming, could be low-cost"

                    "is she vocalizing? is that all she does?"

language not separate adaptation but an internal aspect of
something much wider

human symbolic culture

            without it you die

low-level marketing and publicity Decider has the bright idea of
how to encapsulate his vision of "poetry making"

"Aha," he thinks, *"a lone rocking chair at the edge of an ocean, then you
can make what you will of this desolate nihilism: will she submit?"*

phonemes produced on the outsides of our body

shed skins to be nameless

decided the pipeline that will change the cartography
of living things
deciding the Grand Canyon

hundreds of water bodies threatened

endangered habitat of whooping cranes
pallid sturgeons
decide the future of American burying beetles

decide assault weaponry, blood on hands

decided the model of air, water
of earth
of fire
in
    empire

offer a truced tribunal, tear down the wall or they shake within your
cacophony the end of wilderness

memo: we need a commission for the scrutiny tribunal
Deciders of all accounts
took the stratus off a poet-face (stratus = layer)
kept her in a cage

cumulus more of heap like severance pay
cirrus = mere curl of a hair resembles coil of sound

double bind
decided our debt to one another
was it not *humanitas* & *caritas*?

none of that, they said
those who created a system of amnesia
other gateways, escape hatch
cascade of timeless motion
hiding behind an ambivalent waterfall
a waterfall just falls

faceted elemental tableau
it doesn't notice your paranoia

cloned sisterhoods in the dark castellum

where is our feminism?

your job disturbing the edges?
crying like a mourner
wish she'd disappear that other . . .

nimbus

halo around your words
words like combs, twigs
prowl the low and complicated grasses

as a brick turns to dust
nimbus is relational

nimbus is the older sister

more experienced
hidden
can't shake her
and shadow government

    off

radar

sequence by sequence selling off the genome

Let me explain, the Poet said
no vagaries I hate that you would think that
not knowing but echoing mentor's extant scheme
neither pounce nor sweat nor becoming intentional
the "that" in not knowing her agenda but make the writing clear

would speak of the innovation of poetry
anxious in the wings
as if knowing might spark intimacy
to bring release from knowable things
of this world

impermanence of the altostratus and such

faint beads of sweat staining gossamer robes

altruistic, asymmetrical
altiplano did ascend together?
did we climb the jeweled stair?
or here
did tryst?

as in
transfer and truce
her part in my drama translated,
she was an impostor of the worst order
all landscapes not inviolable
all terrain not off the map

she beat me to the antechamber, and

may I speak of urgency?

spider thread spun
rubble in late fall

she took this man of mine and then she took that one

 It was a time of *Gos* = goose
+ summer
Swedish *sommer trad*
a summer thread

silk goose down

Mädchen Sommer girls' summer

Filmy . . . and took the women too

Alter ego

Bi-locator

Capgras delusion

Clone

Fetch

Ikiryo

Vardøger

struggle for Marriage Equality

and escaped to scope the Tundra

seeing the shape of a monster to come
  she studied these things

Poet did this and then she did that
she didn't really want this or that
but she did it this and that way
anyway for the verbal motion of that
and that movement and motion,
the participial -*ing* for the sake of being in a verb
Decider wanted blood in cunning
and the possibility of poetic emblem, rune, insignia
a symbol—a device—a ruse—of power to hold a master language
together

A world domination, Decider thought
If he could but get the right word or words, he mused, the right
combination of vowel of consonant of phones of phoneme of
melopoeia
and translate them all into every language in the world . . .

he would know . . . he would hold . . . he would prosper

but she withheld her knowledge
and plotted the rescue of the tapes that would be held hostage
my doppelgänger knows not the magic formula of

look closely, the undertaker said:
serpent ring entwined upon itself with ruby eyes,

shapely waist, not as dainty as the others

an amber "stone" the Poet had purchased at the Goddess Conference
that magnetized wary opponents to her cause

The Capgras delusion theory is a disorder in which a person holds
that a friend, spouse, parent, or other close family member has been
replaced by an identical-looking impostor

Cases in which patients hold the belief that time has been warped or
substituted
have also been reported

It occurs most frequently in females

"They have taken her place!"
"I will lock my bedroom door!"

Psychologists have hypothesized that patients with Capgras
delusion may have mirror images of "prosopagnosia"
The conscious ability to recognize faces is intact
but they might have damage
no emotional arousal

This could result in the experience of recognizing someone while
feeling something was "not quite right"

A phantom on my brain
Not quite right

replica, spits image,
facsimile identity
duplicate papers
not quite right
a ghostly counterpart
ghost wife in debt or offered
substitute in old revenge
a double walker

a double goer
left temporoparietal junction
conceptual elaboration kicks in

blue as an iconographic polysemic reading

space = *akasha*
shining and clear
keep it that way please

you out there? in my brain?
wanting to be who you are in the right body
marry the one you love

body against a boundary of space
peripheral vision

bi-location
in need to project a body off my own

let *her* take blame

or credit

   entwine

not quite right

cryogenized?

devices of Moroccan sky and geometry
women cover themselves in hand of caution of curtain
richly adorned
undulate across public space

Jamaa el Fna

dressed like a hippie
one in wig, bell-bottoms, with instrument case
but down under, raging terrorist

not quite right in the Argana Café time machine

impostor you sing of

secret knowledge in the medina

impostors trick
then leave you,
endarkened prison cell, who gets inside
subterranean bondage

tit for tat
I give you "bullet"
    you give me "stash"
I give you numbers
        passwords, key codes
identity papers

people die
more people die

you give out

murder in broad daylight

as I pass through Switzerland
dead faces of their youth
in and on the blunt news and media channels
artifact: a fruit vendor setting himself on fire in Tunisia

The Deciders are concerned about damage control
They are concerned about everything as the day comes to a close
Day's end, they say
"At day's end . . ."
Deciders of the upper echelon are hidden inside towers
and protected by radioactive shields or hunkered down
in caves like secret cities
Deciders send their signals all over the world
They are themselves all over the world
with passwords like "destiny" and "tintinnabulation"
But the lower echelon workaholic Deciders
spend long hours hallucinating an enemy
of flesh, sinew, bone, of poetry and its portents
They will design their clones to be mortal enemies
They will wear the clothes of the superpowers
Dark uniforms with powder-blue helmets
They will create policy upon policy for pepper spray
"Just give them some gunpowder," they say
They could also put a well-dressed provocateur in the
Deciding-Way
In the midst of a situation
"A situation at day's end," they like to say
"in our Deciding-Way"
This is quite a feat, creating and visualizing an enemy:
"A situation at day's end in our Deciding-Way"
You have to have a keen imagination
You study hard to know how to do this,
creating enemies you will need to destroy
What color should they be
Atom by atom you put the enemy together
Giving your factotum gestures and dark poetic substance
Or maybe he/she/it remains invisible
A game in cyberspace
And then you give him some attitude
and he/she/it takes off

He seems to be a player in the spectacle of life
The upper-echelon Decider observes
"Job well done"

It has become quite clear the enemy will progress with attitude and firepower

You can summon any machine to be activated in the Deciding-Way

At the end of the day they always say it's what they really mean that dreadful *"at the end of the day"*

A tombstone, at the end of the day

what use have we of spies and they be hanged for less

look-alikes created
        in order to delude someone into believing
that someone
    actually absent
 is present

        (*reset the electronic security device*)

 for example, a princess appears as wife of Taladhyaja

you see?
her sandals leave no prints . . .
she walks above the ground
carefully, slowly in trance
her sari a sheaf of gold

and this story might circulate
how to beware of her

her theme of illusory "double"
might shake confidence in the uniqueness and solidarity of
her waking persona
jolt her awake

peculiar ambiguity of dream
where the dreamer sees herself
        simultaneously as subject
and as object
the way the soul in limbo watches its own corpse in the Tibetan text

way I touch you, gossamer,
streaks   strands   hair filament
splash in raw daylight
dragonfly
signal of gnat-life
and with light
striation
expands   explodes

further
to complex variant
double of the dreamer who is both author and character behind
    the waterfall

and press against outlying reaches,
splash the boundary of allegory
web of gossamer light
to have a scrim of water separate from the space under the cavern
and outsider worlds
to melt a line between
  observer and observed
  the droplets disperse nearby to replicate the same way again
what lives   is harvested
double in myths   dreams
or illusion between *duplicadas*
walk this earth
shell of emotion
        makes possible witnessing of the dream process
 protects the dreamer
from dangers of complete solipsism
of enclosing herself in a world
        in which she is the only citizen

the living living
living living living living
the living living dreaming dreaming
dead dead walking living dreaming dead living
the living thread

and in the laboratory grow life
with a glint of DNA
"I am the only one at day's end," the Poet might say

dream double combats solipsism
by providing a second person to serve
working her way out of nothing
as a corroborating authority

but that person is another aspect of the dreamer and does not
combat the logic of solipsism

impossible to surmount
her arm an arc of water air earth fire
face-to-face combat

bootstrap logic? pull her up out of the watery mirror

and we have our magic replications

duplications' reflections

the wise text says:

sorrow will not bring enlightenment
the sage will try scripture
the sage will try illustration
the sage will transform into a new woman
to mouth these words

I went to play my lute for Decider Vishnu
and found him engaged in erotic play
　　　with wife Lakshmi
and when he saw me he had her vanished

I have conquered illusion

but you can't say this you can't say I have conquered illusion
no one, not even the gods
may conquer illusion

I beg you Vishnu show me what illusion is

he took me to a beautiful pond and invited me to bathe in it
I entered the pool as Vishnu instructed and became woman

this is illusion, he said

a master of erotic skills
made love to me night and day
lost all sense of time
drinking wine
rapt in pleasure
twelve years a single moment

I forgot my former body
and life as a sage

eight sons many grandchildren later
I was happy—no—couldn't name my sorrow

lot of a woman
I bred I bred

estranged not-come-to-joy
reads-many-books
went to know the world as a woman
ask a woman, ask others
women had tenderer thought?
is it not a gentler feeling for the world?

one day an enemy attacked

    family all dead I rage wept I fled

lot of a woman they said
weaker weaker woman

Decider Vishnu came to me
why are you so sad?
remember what I said
this is delusion

who are you and whose bodies are these strewn about?

perform the rituals for the dead
you are not what you seem
this is not what it seems
in the allegorical dimension of your struggling text

went to the lake called "Male-Ford"

glanced in, saw a text of light

(pumtirtha)

It said:
You had millions of sons who died in
life
    after life

millions of husbands and fathers too
    for whom you grieve

it is all a mistake and arises in your own mind as a dream

I entered the ford and instantly became a man
    with a lute in my hand
I remembered I was a transformer in the Patriarchy

I sang:
as a woman I experience the misery of worldly existence
as a man I create more suffering
om ah ah
experience in the illusory world is a nightmare
    from which one wishes to escape

[*Preservation metadata is a subset of administrative metadata aimed at supporting the long-term retention of digital objects. It overlaps with technical and administrative metadata, detailing important information about the digital file, including any changes in the file over time and management history. The object meant to be preserved by preservation metadata is the preservation master digital object itself. Preservation metadata need not be created for the Analog object or derivative copies created for access purposes. In the case of complex digital objects, one preservation metadata record will be created to describe the entire complex object.*

The management of the full range of metadata is through the Metadata Encoding Transmission Standard which provides a structure for encoding descriptive, structural metadata . . . etcetera.]

The spectacle under suspicion. The gaze under suspicion. Orality is feminine.

The Deciders abjure feminism.

sorrow enlightens, they say
sorrow knows no boundary
sorrow: an acerbic archival wilderness
sorrow penciled in red
a direction in my book of prayer

apocalyptic vehicle
interstellar vehicle
intertextual
intertidal
intertwined

but I would intervene
and call myself intervenient
an intervenient vehicle

convenient in sorrow

    a lurid interruption
someone who lurks
waiting to spring to life

prognostic,
and needing escape
   tears that splash and are a running mate in all endeavors

but this illusory world is also sensuous and joyous and intangible

as a woman I drank wine and ate forbidden things

intoxication to distract the Original Anne

a plot on imagination, a romp through time and gender

as a wifeless sage,

or wandering singer who carries a lute

another version:

the sage emerges from the water
on the occasion
of his transformation
　　from woman
　　into man
he still holds his woman-hand above the water

it remains the hand of a woman holding a succulent fruit

he dives back into the water immerses his hand
turning into the hand of a man holding a lute

when the sage leaves the world of illusion,
a perishable memory turns a hard enduring lute

who decides reverie in the russet castellum
 can force your dreams in their time/space machine

    as I went to bathe in a lake I morphed

I came out on the bank as a woman among women

when they asked me who I was I said, *woman*
              I think woman among women

who I am where I come from and how do I have the form of a
woman

 I have no idea

I left my male form but woman I think woman among women
            is deception a pronoun?

Vishnu picked up my lute and went away
I forgot my former body

a king came by he married me

"she whose face is her fortune"

down with kings who decide magic
flavor my desire
a twist where we talk

we joke about language modules
and make love on the road
I could be created out of twigs and dirt
as he puts in the mechanical apparatus

the world is full of Deciders
I've always felt and say it such again

the world has to change for true identity (love) to burn

she sent a message to the Base, *whatever you do to me know this*

I know this from Derrida

Archive is shelter
Archive is the disembodied voice of a palpable consciousness
Archive is a jumbled dream
Archive needs poetry you must never forget
Archive is inscription
Archive is aspiration
Archive tells many stories
I am archon
and a mere inscripted postcard is Archive
when we return to our speech
and start our own country
take this as directive:
memory of an animal is also yours
Archive all opposable thumbs we have record of
and many wisdom identities
Archive's murmur circulates around the room
Archive lets originals breathe
you can't tamper with Archive
it's a strange cosmology
Archive is antithesis to a war on memory and stealing of poet fire
Archive is the tender footprint
Archive will not tread on the footprints of the most vulnerable
Archive is a trust
let Archive record the names of those going out of this world
Tristan Albatross
all disappeared
all suicided
Archive listens into the margins
Archive is a privileged topology

Archive exists as a map of the future beyond the exigencies of
electronic media which has transformed the relative reality of *Homo
sapiens sapiens*

if you are good at this, please memorize
are you good at this?
memorize Archive
Archive could be safe from composite strife

[*Gain Intellectual Control of the Collection.*
Consider cassette tape life expectancy.
Water pipes run through storage space: materials are housed in a
100-year floodplain with environmental swings, no climate control.
Security: multiple keys to storage exist, the space is not secured—walls
that leave space at ceiling height can be easily breached.
Digital collections on CDs which are at risk themselves due to disc failure
and equipment obsolescence. . . .]

Archive is housed by, and reanimates sentient beings
Archive is nest, is house, is reverie
Archive will hold you
"And the line comes (I swear it) from the breath . . ."
Archive is aubade, is alba, is Tagelied
is seduction
is Mnemosyne
Archive is dying and Archive is not dying
who lives to push the buttons to install the implants of Archive?
a far agent, a forest, a mountain to climb, an orange sunset,
a cloth for the body
strong ropes to circle and carry
dynamite with an App for soil content,
an App to read constellations in the sky
moon a fingernail above you is a modest proposal

sometimes a wildebeest on the tundra remembers a former life
and an albatross crossed your shadow at sea one day
Tristan whose name means sadness quested the Grail
and drank a love potion

This is the sublimated test of future identity

always felt a brain to be
fluctuating syntagma

a syntactic/semantic processing
semantic as in being brain-and-consciousness-awake

syntax as sister to succession, a superstition

do I have control in scenario? do I love my mission in life?

scenario: where they lock me up and take my poems from me
and make undue mockery and travesty of Original Anne
and control her life span

maybe she's object of jealousy

open surgery in a theater of observation

scalpel coming down

I feel like the scream of a cyborg
as I watch my archival consciousness threatened

as the spirit struggles for survival

whisper that would cause a drop in the water table
no single river flows to the sea

whisper that traverses the braided river
as a tribal uprising might clash your civilization again

no leisure from the Deciders who take up so much of your attention
getting into the airwaves again
what brain will access that dangerous frequency?

no leisure from deciding
the worth of everyone
the dollar value of intellectual property
try to love within a system
survive the within: of being within system
gap in the charts,
life force dipped down yet still within itself a system

acts of marauding identity theft
will threaten life span of poetry

by gossip you get the story
a cautionary tale, amnesia

include: *Lycaenidae*

About 6,000 species worldwide
whose members are known as the "gossamer-wing'ed butterflies"

The blues (*Polyommatinae*)

The coppers (*Lycaeninae*)

The hairstreaks (*Theclinae*)

And the harvesters (*Miletinae*)
all still extant because well hidden in planet-life

Some larva are capable of producing vibrations and low sounds that
are transmitted through the substrates they inhabit. They use these
sounds to communicate with ants.

Adult individuals often have hairlike tails complete with black-and-
white annulated appearance. Many species also have a spot at the

base of the tail and some turn around to confuse potential predators from recognizing the "true head" orientation.

Ants have their own systems but receive survival "calls."

These are signals to be collegial

she thought about her station in life.
did she understand the metaphorical *duplicada*
and the philosophy as crepuscular which is fragile by definition?
ruse or trick of time to use her body and form as . . . Poet?

she would visit Chasm Falls
climb East Desolation Peak
she would scout for a safe haven to house all hope and fear

or did she aspire beyond station what she'd been born to . . .

flicker of it,
"place"
      out, out of it
fragility, the joke about past lives
the hunting of the golem, stick and mud effigy
as when she first looked at a corpse
someone she had loved
wanting, watching as his body flamed
 to smear ashes over her own body
  ashes that were once steady arms
 held her fast
sturdy legs of a body
twisted around her
    a flame coiled at the center, below
as he enters her
  dare speak of a face?
  they were exceedingly young
she said, becoming one together
like a cargo cult of magical thinking

dark curls
     saliva

l feel like a suttee widow
long hours at the Ganges
looking out on the water
devotees come to bathe
collect the drops of polluted water now
        still sacred in the imagination
lineage of sacral tears

thrice toss these oaken ashes in the air . . .

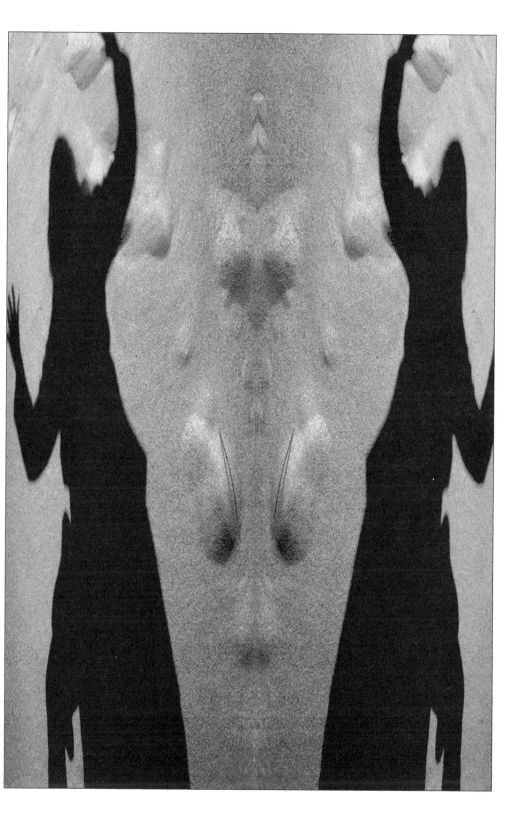

watch the flames on the ghats
dart like insects to the sky
a night sky this time
smoke coils like dragons,
sea serpents, or seeing the skeleton of a phantasmagorical airship
ascend through clouds

she put the ashes of her mentor in the duplicated river Tirta Gangga
spectacle of death
a phantom skull at the breast
gleam, did she kill her shadow?
polished bone—color of raven's wings—turned
to blackest coral—at the breast
might still gleam

or the hollow sockets once his grand old poet eyes
wasted in spectral identity?

co-opted in a ghoulish meditation
how an impostor might coalesce
and enter when your mind is weak
turn away from it
but you know
how demons enter
backward
facilitating the extinction
of the Zoe Waterfall Damsel

she might set it down, all extinctions
would they be of any use in her prism

bringing events to order? *backward*

she saw masses of fabrication in the stories others tell
saw through claims and exaggerations
saw through protests of love, fealty
 way a daughter might, skeptic
   of "history" might

especially "his" or rather a "his" might
or big sister or mother or "hers"

 being ahistorical
see spectacle as separation, spectacle as end of our linguistic aid

a "mistress narrative," you might say, perhaps preferable
  subtle   persuasive
insistently oral

                most melodious tone

studied other languages on foreign language tapes
spent time in the prison library

an auspicious time
up against uncertain worlds
shrinking
where human is finite, an invention of recent date
time that we say our fantasies are controlled by propaganda
born too into the middle of a century before
   we are "gone"
or when the mores changed and
favored women who were set up against each other
   in jealous rage
that too passes . . . will pass

may allegory speak of unconditional love?

I want to amuse you, my doubles, hasty beloveds
come wash all your thoughts upon me,
a seed-vault sanctuary on a remote sea

a living casket Porsephina keeps of Archive
old romances, antic lore, and scrutiny take over,
considered the centuries she had been born to cross
in crossing of millennium
twin broken vertebrae
interminable time, it seemed
growing
to archonhood . . .
what she was willing to part with
let go of
who lets go of
shed more skins
why she would go out as one one day
go out as another one the next
looking into the darkness of her own time
with congruent vision
artifact: a silenced vibration in your pocket
cause for alarm?

the other Anne took to the stage

she did imitations of the Original Anne

she billed herself Anne

she went public all over the world
    with all the attributes and the albatross of Original Anne

she had some high notes

she could sing in a queer falsetto

and occasionally some deep tones like Tibetan monks
    which Original Anne had so perfected

deep tones that reverberated with the earthy guttural sounds of
    Original Anne

she claimed to have read and know all the books read and studied
    by the Original Anne

because they were of the same historical time frame she would
    attach signifying herself to the signs and sighs of the Original Anne
    eidolons of Original Anne

she mounted her telescope to the coordinating points and
    frequencies of Original Anne

the other Anne knew that if there were debt it could never be paid
    in full
  to the Original Anne

the other Anne was enjoying her fame and wealth

she scattered gold coins in the paths of her followers

she would stop and turn then toss the coins
    and the followers no longer noticed Original Anne

coins dropped from the other Anne with a genuine-sounding sound
    a powerful sound of empty value

money would replace Original Anne

. . . sculpting of Jupiter's gossamer rings by its shadow . . . this was another reach in her investigation of the nature of gossamer, light-years away . . .

. . . as dust near Jupiter is produced when interplanetary impactors collide energetically with small inner moons and dust is organized into a main ring, an inner halo, and two fainter and more distant double gossamer rings . . .

. . . as when dust grains alternately charge and discharge when traversing shadow boundaries, allowing the planet's powerful magnetic light to excite orbital eccentricities and inclinations as well. . .

. . . as when dust in the gossamer rings originates essentially in the same way as that in the main ring and halo. Its sources are the inner Jovian moons Amalthea and Thebe. High-velocity impacts by projectiles coming from outside the Jovian system eject dust particles from their surfaces. These particles initially retain the same orbits as their moons but then gradually spiral inward by Poynting-Robertson drag. The thickness of the gossamer rings is determined by vertical excursions of the moons due to their nonzero orbital inclination . . .

Observable properties of the rings: rectangular cross section, decreases of thickness in the direction of Jupiter, and brightening of the top and bottom edges of the rings.

Some properties go unexplained. Like the Thebe extension, which may be due to unseen bodies outside Thebe's orbit, and structures visible in the back-scattered light. One possible explanation of the Thebe extension is the influence of the electromagnetic forces from the Jovian magneto-sphere.

There could be two particle populations in the gossamer rings; one slowly drifts in the direction of Jupiter while another remains near a source moon trapped in 1:1 resonance with it.

. . . "back-scattered light" is the light scattered at an angle close to 180° relative to solar light . . .

Observable properties of the effect of gossamer rings on consciousness moving in parallel circles and may never embrace.

> appear, dissolve, ~~canceled~~
> a model for musing

in the treasure trove of Mnemsyne

a movie of your spiraling memory

After the taking of the castle turning it to a prison through antics of deception and dream there had been some change in their selves, in the twinned psychological weather. There had been a shift whether *she she* would respond violently or *she she* would be serene or metabolically charged to move about, and we saw them, moving about with a kind of joy. . . . No, begin again. . . .

Had you heard why did you hear and what did you hear or what did they let you hear? That one Decider was a creationist, that another was a misogynist.

That the Deciders may imprison one of you. I was already that one.

There was something there. The twins in our lives. A twitter about the doubles in our lives and imprisonment. And using one to conquer the other and steal her magic.

They might confuse themselves
in the Decider Device of Double Annes
And the care to the students that would not be given
And the care to Archive that would not be proffered

Breath quickens, arms flail . . . there were warnings. How *she she* would appear suddenly at mealtime in a wrench of remorse, mumbling about aviary sightings and how a wing might be a portent of doom if slightly askew. And *she she* would also be fine looking up at the stars from the fortress tower. Portents from light-years away.

Arrived and not quite arrived.

Auguries of mixed-message victory.

Or studying birds and the entrails of birds.

And the reading of the entrails was such that Original Anne would survive but struggle and she would have to escape to a place to hide her cache in a place they called "Diamond Vault" or "Inside Wings of Butterflies."

In the meantime . . . crouch and wait, small binoculars in hand. Walk the prison yard. A special dispensation to her scientific obsession. A fleet swallow. Pika sightings too—skittish, you remember, on the tundra. Dusk. Then you want to get down and pray up here, someone was overheard saying. And that she did get down in front of a form, the form of a Madonna, an elderly woman who seemed, as her car license indicated, from Nebraska, I always observed where they were from. Up again brushing the matter, glacial middens from knees. Twins are happier on the open road. Yes, twins are happier on the folksy road. She thought of the dark castellum and how relieved to be almost free of that unhappy mind.

Liberated from a strange and compromised nightmare.

She was a founder, had they forgotten?
The other was riding her coattails through the labyrinths of Samsara.

Wizened stooped Original Anne would crouch down. *How could you not keep company with death in such a world?* she'd say.

The other Anne: *It's early on in the century and we'll look back at our folly and be amused.* She, youthful other, clone of sister, twin in phobias and wayward plans.

Original Anne who was one with the constant lustrations, a devotee in practice of cleansing, she was wearing a heart on a sleeve a tourniquet on a sleeve a house on a sleeve a survival tome on sleeve. It will not be amusing.

She she was one to remark upon this at length as *she she* said it the problems of *our new and early century* as if that would obviate desire and put a fine point on it all. And eschew a totality of responsibility.

Where are you from?

The void, both *shes* would say.

Speak of cold storage, speak of the delicate plants, the Indian paintbrush just one, close to the Divide.

The Divide between Deciders of ego and malice and ignorance, and those who do not chose to pluck this humble flower.

They exchanged places for a cryptic moment
Original Anne felt the dead pulse of the Deciders' Anne
Then a hurricane then humming then humility
Joke about the tides in our bodies, the monthly motion and dip in
mood, impressions in failure etched,
affinities, delineations of going down
Down where?

Dear Original Anne: I will tell you this in writing and you may
respond. More memos for the mind, begging response in the middle
of the night, flaming e-mails by the light of a pallid moon . . .

The sadness from the other side of the wall . . .
I imagined the room

Bare, but of essentials made . . .

The writing book, a ledger star-crossed, archival items that find
home here

A legend
I imagined a tomb for your holdings, a pyramid, a sepulchre, a vault

I can track your every move
I am your virus or your inventor

I see your thoughts you will travel as you desire where to go, move
through walls

I could breathe love into you a perfect fabrication
A competition?

I could breath now

A foil

Who is most controlling and vile in our overworked world?

Original Anne kept silent but nurtured her own counsel:
I'm studying the tundra now, as a diamond tomb
Its subtle form its very chill environment might contain, condense,
preserve . . .

a line of poetry brings language again to language
startling in its brevity
magic on the head of a pin
microdots of inwardly spiraling space and time

How small things survive under harsh conditions, a metaphor for all
your paranoia will be answered. Investigate storms and the tempest
of ice high on this shelf at the end of the world. Conflagrations set by
angry insouciant campers. How often will the sun bake your thoughts
to hardened clay? How will you be broken and fight back?

In this brief digital age, never destroy the original singularities, voice
recognitions that might haunt your sleep. How do they hibernate
through coming millennia, how translate into your own thought
forms so you have access to a time when what gathered in your brain
emulated the progress of a voice over time, its poetry and desire, and
when the images still held power of what was now waning

How might I get there, how may I go there. What might I accomplish
there? How does the chemical in my brain translate to this hiberna-
tion which is in itself a sign of barren ground
Elegies must not be cynical and poets must travel

She and her double walked through the souk down the path, put her arm out toward one of the Deciders (in white and gold djellaba), as if to point him out, expose him, and crouched down . . . Deciders were everywhere now . . . across the globe . . . a powerful Archive could have portal to the stars . . . the known universe. . . . a megatheater of sound

"across wounded galaxies . . ."

"belly of our reward . . ."

She and her shadow crouched . . .

as disembodied voices of Archive sent jolts of consciousness through the megasphere . . .

". . . a sweeping revision . . ."

". . . embers of the rain . . ."

"the judge was the wind let the old things take over . . ."

"Truancy of will where she let it fall"

"Door unlocked after the wounding . . ."

"Thinking is not worrying . . ."

"I made this book of sonnets . . ."

"I, an island, sail . . ."

"I'm so in love with art that it will get me into the next world . . ."

Ceramic day, as if djinns activated the sound waves

The child indicated . . . joy in the vibrating atmosphere

"first there were the FIRST PEOPLE . . ."

. . . something there—sod . . . no . . . turn it over . . . something odd and human

A tessera a shatter a glove a fragment, old shoe

"Where human feet can squish the daylights out of cowering anemone . . ."

"People are so like what they wear . . . especially on their . . . exteriors . . . ?"

She and her double looked at the child who said this, version of herselves too young to understand what she was saying, bound in her little souk world, but it wasn't so important, although she made effort. *The child was deaf,* her nursemaid said . . .

They stopped putting a few coins in the Amazigh musician's cloth as he played the gambri . . .

What do you sing of?

. . . subtle difference between loss . . . life . . . custom. . . .

loss . . . mourning

"I met Death—he was a sportsman . . . "

His partner under her veil was fully absorbed in the music, synchronous with every lilt and turn "the beauties of the Levant when we had them"

". . . not all the works of Mozart worth one human life . . ."

"a place so hip even the rats doing the hustle . . ."

A child could not hear but felt rhythm of the night and throng of bodies crossing, recrossing in public space

What I found, she said . . . reaching down holding it up, *what I found—cassette!*—they were still familiar items in the old market. Obviously the child knew . . . she wanted to hear it play *but she was deaf*, her nursemaid said . . .

She smiled instead and looked away . . . sentences were not located in time for her . . .

"think of what needs to be what needs to be"

Anne Anne the Escaped said something as she tried to explain, and then Anne Anne the Escaped ran into the riad down the alley
                        toward her shelter . . . a small cell of reticulation . . .

she and *she* entered the place of volumes of books, beautifully bound in Moroccan leather *she* and *she* had been referring to in endless investigation escaping toward Tundra. Unfinished pages and notes, notes, all useless . . . looking into calibrations . . . but from where and toward what . . . how long do you measure desire or worrying accoutrements of the archival desk. . . . I, Original Anne, *hate all this!*

Original Anne thought of Ashurbanipal, *his* library. The civilized Gilgamesh and wild Enkidu. The ancient astronauts and the out-of-place artifacts. It was 10,000 BCE. She thought of Marduk and his fifty names, a lot of identity to keep track of . . .

She thought of all the Deciders in a Free-Market World. How they relegated the Archive as if in a metaphor of car-dealing or house shares . . .

all the muscles toward this moment to explode

feeling herself to . . . implode . . . touch herself in poetry . . .
        to implode

rend the veil

crack the mirror

in this wilderness of stone . . .

a salty poet-tear fell on a page—were both troubled?

who of them was allowed to cry? when would she be released?

watch the droplet morph with ink and then blur
with her imagination

of that

shift . . . water to matter

to e.phem.e.ra—*le point ephémère* . . .

where things begin and end
and die
and continue.

dot in space

uncontrollably into something . . . the Original Anne cried out—

why doesn't everyone . . . just bug off?

Anne the Only now rose to prominence in her further "self" deception
Original went into retreat but I'll be back she said . . .
Only had a public voice
Anne the Only gave an opinion about forgiving and forgetting
Only was tongue-in-cheek
She was being photographed
A dynamic spread on the entire discordant culture of the 20th and
    early 21st century
        with references to works of art and photography, to the memes
        of dance and theater and film
There was still some interest in the bygone days
which continued to stagger along
Her many surrounding assistants took care of this,
shuffling around her, huffing and puffing around her
and arranging all the artifacts of the last century around her body
the body of Anne Only

And when she was photographed Only concentrated her gaze on
something very small but very close at hand
    with particular eaglelike scrutiny

What could that something be?
It was an exceedingly fine and miniature replica of Original Anne.
She held it in her hand, it was a doll a totem, a hologram

It came to life, aging forward and de-cohering backward

Only Anne had control

check those items at the gate
and be sure to compartmentalize all they decide on you
be sure to secure all your ointments in plastic
be sure your relics are quite in order with the proper documents of
    provenance

Only Anne was quite decidedly a deciding one so there was no
desire for Original to speak or remotely consider deciding
you could be a simulacrum that becomes Only and Deciding too.

Only sent Original into the arena to represent her as spectacle
where she could be enlarged at will, touch the icon on the screen.
The way the famous artist had sent a doppelgänger as a stand-in
to a faraway port in a faraway city where they were not accustomed
to impostors and they had rarely seen photographs or copies of the
original.

wanted to tear it all down . . .

give way
        the fortress less claustrophobic now in her mind
escape artist in a hatched plan cooked up by all the advocates,
helpers in the uterine castellum

The Stay and Sees and Listening Ones, eyes and ears of this and
future lives

at standstill her heart but run quickly now they cautioned
time going in an opposite direction in all disguise
toward another body, your shadow running amok

        and to skies?

1. sail directly before the wind to safety
2. do not offer identification but keep
   valid in a given area a run of notes away from captivity
3. you can quickly leap forward or climb upward
4. give up all ambition in your identity captivity narrative

they had "allowed" her to escape out on the route of Archive
"go see, go see the destruction of your poetry world
all its rhizomes, autonomous zones"

"put out your memory"

never she said, *never*

with this trove in my ear

Never

remembering a time when she would have said this is dream
this is rook
this is crook

and thought of the others—those *voices*—and of the things in that
shoe box on that site in that shed on that floodplain

or in a room without climate control in a room with walls not up to
the ceiling on that floodplain

fires licking at the fringes of town, coming up over mountains onto
that floodplain,
evacuation orders in hand

is there a plan? I'll make one

the periscope not meant to be, its serial number rusted because it
   had fallen in a pool of water

you catch the drift, "feverish red mist"

something numeric to escape from

Original Anne in her continuing bondage now floating above
   the Distraction World

they let her out on a short leash, assuming she would lead them
to the
original Archive

fathoms deep in her and in the ground

she claimed ignorance
she strapped on her Byronic clubfoot
hoping to be well hidden inside a life-form resembling
a ring of daisy, a ring of mushroom, ring of aspen, ring of stone

examine slice of tundra under a microscope
how to surpass wind and bitter cold if you were Archive of paper
and magnetic tape
artifact awaiting transference to the multiverse
analogue or digital or
unobtrusive subtle trace—implant—in the brain cloud. . . .

I digress . . .

In retrospect, she was and is always mentioned by someone or other I love or made love with as someone I resembled, and as I took this into account in my technology of inscription, in my technology of audio implant as I had questions, many questions, questions of her life, her life-in-mind and her life as one-who-played-so-many-others, as if in entropy of a death drive one might say she kept the roles coming, so many to keep up with, so many others of myself as I resembled her. So many troubled Poet others. "I" as phantom or "function," I as "factotum," or I as poet in my anterior, subversive, poet-structured activity, and many possible ulterior roles inspired by hers. Think of them. Count them, many to keep track of. Conglomerations of seductive tendencies, dangerous tendencies, where paper, cardboard, and ribbon is not your game. Rage. Heartbreak. Edgy. A sob-sister not your game. A heartbreaker might be. A gun, a dagger, three furious volcanoes inside. A confused movie persona inside. Emanating a specter of myself that fills her show, fills her screen, fills her shoe—I ask what size is she. That was my first question. Eight, eight and a half, narrow, I'd guess. They look—those bodies and parts of bodies we project so much upon—larger on-screen than they naturally are. And it's interesting to guess when you see a body in a doorway, when you see a body in a street, when you see the body in a market in an open doorway in liminal space walk across a room and sit down or open a door, hand on the brass doorknob, what is the measurement of the rest of the architecture to that hand to that body to that face not to mention the dimensions of the room itself to body. Angles of relational strife. Someone figuring it all out behind the lens. Or stand-ins. They have to be similar in size. Especially in bed or naked, slaughtered on a floor. They might be creating smaller furniture for this very purpose. False props. Simulacra. They might ask the leading man to stand on a box to lift his height to proffer a kiss. And of her dress size I wonder. Not a twelve, which I have been now and then and sometimes eight, but tall and thin, an eight I'd say, an eight but tall eight. Or six, definitely a six. A narrow bust. Yes, six. Walking down a sandy beach, narrow hips, and she over sixty, that's what I like, I was confessing just now, sexy over sixty. Another question was, Were there any Mongolian epicanthic folds in her genetic history? A Capgras delusion, a doppelgänger syndrome? Comrade. Interlocutress. Mover and shaker. Poet. Create institutions and watch them dissolve. As a djinn might.

not your game not your game
a strained stalemate or a computer of lesser advantage

not your game

a destitute metabolism
or empty mummy cartonnage,
not your game not your game
not your gain
but scorching Fire?

All my life ones I love as I was saying comparing me to her and just last week one saying again when I had been in public space and done something publicly, oh you look so much like her do you know that? Your eyes and neck. And he had seen me in private space, and said that before, some years back, like her, like her. Your back, that was it, backing up now. A tattered tux, a uniform, a glamourous Italian wife of a terrorist, or plain young wife. Acting them out, sometimes with her neck in my mind. Rotten to the core, a girl with a George in her title, a young woman with Oz in her title. Boyish. Someone impish, someone testing you, provoking you to do some damage, or you might be someone (this is a difficult role now) who is with someone who just walks away. Disappears. Why? He had said, another he-I-loved-once had said—you resemble her neck, or perhaps I wasn't hearing it right, or "what a neck, so much like hers—" as if he knew her. And he said, "Your hair, your hair resembles hers." Another he-I-loved-once had acted many roles and loved many actresses; that's what we called them in our early years, "tresses." And then he married one, a real one. There was a role now in memory to absorb and as I sat there thrilled, I was her neck, I was her hair, her slanted eyes, I was the color of her hair. I was not alone, a woman-alone-dreaming-of-stardom, because I had stardom, her acting the roles for me because he said, "You don't follow the money"—was he implying that she did? A different klieg light and a pace, a voice, the way she lights the cigarette. I close my eyes now and visualize her. I know her. She does not follow the money.

Another question has to do with sex, the story of her real-in-life *ménage à trois*. I'll back off here again. I've never exactly lived in a *ménage à trois*, although there was a very close friendship or would you say entanglement with two men at once and one had a crush on the other the one who was with me and maybe I had been with this one before I was with the one I stayed with many years. We were what you might say carefree. We lived in the country where new mountains jut up from primal matter. Where tundra was ocean once, you may collect shards of seashells fourteen thousand miles above the sea. We drove together in an old truck. We all took peyote in the woods in an act of sympathetic magic ritual for a friend in a coma; and then because of that more psychic inscription and I am still wired after all these years. He's dead now that one I have mourned most of all my dead ones. How you might mourn:

> with a whisper
> with intended circumscribed solace
> on premises with rare and active books,
> with other visceral documents
> with care, devotion
> you take the person's former light in your hands
> you pour it over your face
> you stir your being in the richness of ashes of those you love, loved, will love
> and to death that is evaporating as a murmur is

> I was discreet wanting not to know much about her private life, and I didn't or it would spoil the illusion of she as other, as double I might get my psyche in trouble

> She was going to take me over perhaps,
> From the other side of the wall

> you dedicate yourself as literary executor, as archivist

you read every word as a sign as a "light in your hands"
you became more famous as you die
you plan to rescue all your favorite words from oblivion
lappet   *radiolarium*   *thallophyte*   *quiddity*

this explains, expands, and foliates a temper for your time
the public case grows . . . glaciers melting

Tundra once was ocean. These lush meadows you see where the buffalo roamed and prong horned antelope gamboled now shift in their identity. Could be a future spectacle for the State to muse upon, as citizens hoard candles and water for what they call "The Metabolic Long Haul."

Simulacrum. I didn't call the exorcist. Simulacrum, I didn't call the Thought Police. Simulacrum, I was happy in her aura in her diadem in her orbit. Taught me distance, taught me humility. I might retaliate on myself some injury accorded by an act of shame or frivolity. I don't want her to be frivolous. I want my fabricant to read deep in literature and she plays that writer maybe my favorite role of hers the one who . . . yes, I've already hinted the plot. Urgency and rescue and subterfuge and hide and retrieve. Obviate and destroy the regulations of the Deciders. Let's try to be creative. A writer of novels. Page 1: How did she type that very first take of the scene when she was eviscerated? That was another question. The circular aspect of what she was writing was straight enough, but how did the character the writer behind the movie decide, or did she as actor decide and had the leeway to type whatever she wanted, or with pen. Please don't say poetess. I don't mind actress. But poet is my life. Not right now. Because one has that freedom of tresses, of abandon. *Ess* activates in stress and the movies I appear in. In *The Edge* I play an introspective but ignorant woman who walks by the beach and whose husband is an activist, maybe even qualifies as a terrorist, part of a plot to assassinate a president. This character does not know what is going on. I, wife, never take my clothes off—shy?—when we go to bed in the scene in our little home by the ocean in Deal, New Jersey. There was taking my shirt off, my breasts are naked in *Brand X* opposite you, the one I played this scene with who was one who said earlier I resembled her. But I don't think you had met her yet. Then. Had you? That was another question. Then you went away and eventually married another one who plays roles, one of her best being one, a glamorous one, who cracks up—it's a biopic. Another connected to those who travel to outer space. Once she the true one, my familiar, my other who lovers say resembles me, she the object of my obsession and she the object of their obsession and their attraction to me-as-her obsession and doppelgänger (and I have to ask, do they visualize her when they are with me?) who I address here, the one on whom I focus my attention to eyes and neck and back who ramps up the tension in real life or movie life said, "To discover what is normal, you need to surf a tide of weirdness."

Simulacrum, the next level. She should be more beneficent. If she has money she should help others in the allegory.

[Jamaa el Fna was saved by the grace and lobbying of Juan Goytisolo; that's another story and his. Our night on the town, Marrakech, the other double wore a wig to be like me. The men around us thought she was my daughter.]

Or when I would mount the stage to perform. And she was on the other side of this, performing as well. How did her rhythms resound with mine? Someone might do a graph of our voices and perform "voice recognition."

Would we ever know? *[There is no way to search for information quickly; it is unwieldy and out of date.*

A dedicated, purpose-built studio space would be ideal. Barring that, a small, office-sized room can be adapted for this purpose. The room should be quiet with no obtrusive external noises. Leakage of sound from the studio to adjoining spaces is also a consideration . . . The room should not be square. A rectangular room, with the ceiling height different than the wall lengths, should be used.]

On a mission to scan what she considered valuable to poets, Archive of exploration, and of course let's call out all doubles, the copiers, those that digitize the originals . . .

Or those that usurp *poethic* power.

Sitting here in a quiet house far away from a city. I do this too occasionally, get away to write. Like the lady novelist. Border line of prim cover and seething sex underneath. Was it all three of them, she the duchess and one a model and one a . . . what was she? I digress . . .

A plot to save the world.

Many identities blur in celluloid. Many others also had questions of her. I only wondered because we were close in age and of that time. Her father was a NATO commander; that interested me. Fathers-in-war, daughters-of-the-long-ago-heroic-war. And then I was in the ladies-of-the-night scene in another movie filmed in Quebec with its red silk wallpaper and brothel vibe and playing it in red bra, a feather boa and my line—I made it up, unscripted as it were—was "I'd rather be home reading a good book," and something about my red Tibetan Buddhist protection cord. "What does it protect you from?" "One's own ego" . . . did I say that? And later that same time when we were alone he said it too—"What does it protect you from?"—he another I loved—and also he said, *You look so much like her*. I was sure he had met her by then. He lived near Hollywood and was one of the most famous people in the world.

stardom, stolen?

stretch until you cannot snap back?

I had come to her rooms waiting a shape to investigations
                    I, twice of impetus
and the things in her world so much like mine, intervenient
      maize and pulque
                    firewater and couscous
large photograph of a seashell, djinn in the corner,
Arabic alphabet primer on the desk

a double I, twice of emphasis

                    distant friends . . . it might be easier seeing them in their
elements . . . or thought so . . .
have you walked the tundra yet in this protest?

so we look compelled
or ~~canceled~~ and build the vault for our oristry

catacombs become a choice & enter
Islam Istrokan Xtian and long Byzantine tomes in defense of icons

walk through walls, as Djuna does
saying how love becomes the deposit of the heart
like tidings in a tomb, *bow down*

the dead can do this in their *bardo*, travel through walls
and guide their voices in fierce orality

One of the Deciders sitting in a big boardroom down below:
  "It's all about impermanence anyway, so why the fuss?"

Then this one room for elegizing, mourning fallen icons, emotional
color, disengaged but vital enrichment . . . voice . . . metallic . . .
shine . . . band of light . . . mica-light . . . granular . . . clone that lies
here . . . other side of wall . . . chamber . . . separation . . .
bend . . . eyes aside, or turn right at you caught aside . . .
now . . . cloth . . . texture, inner thinking . . .
of you you might fold under can't put a label on it . . . as we
hope . . . alas I hope, meant because you can have your modesty you
can have me too—so I look . . . cinematic

a rabbit's foot, Rosicrucian cross, a vial of Ganges water, ashes of
the celebrated poet in an oatmeal can

and we look

over all the clutter and shot . . . . shot . . . . shot

through.

of artificial machination
dislocation of a twinned body, extensions,
ashes are remnants of our auspicious time shot shot through
with heat

sprinkle here, anoint my own corpse

double girl, bury your artifacts here

the Original Anne on the runway
the Original Anne "such promise" the Original naive but
awakening to her purpose

Original Anne down for the triple count
Original Anne on the lam
dying to revive

(Anne Only took over all the engagements of the Original Anne
she intercepted her mail, accessing her own demise)

she had sprung her out of the dark castle
now lead me to the tundritic Archive
and commanded: now write this down, your adventure,
your confession for all to see

But Original Anne felt her perspicacity her stamina her purpose return as the power of the Deciders weakened, and she was fully reconstituted. There was an archival tape with aboriginal sticks from Fuji playing in her head, accompanying a poem of terrific orality, and as it played, she felt herself "shaken back" into being.

She stared down the false Anne, a fierce tiger light emanating from her eyes, piercing the deceptive One's resolve. And this diminishing fabricant disappeared, like gossamer, fleeting ephemera on the horizon.

horama . . . oneiros . . . chrematismos . . .

that too, a piracy

her eyes had the glint of Djuna's mind

tortoise shells, sawfish teeth, rock salt, octopus bones,
panther skeleton
skulls and hooves . . . imagine

that they lie at the surface, almost violent
exoskeleton of self's selves

support

and age and Deciders
in contractual . . .
and death

as antlers do a

shot   shot   shot

a simplification is as a war cry

"don't ban poetry from this room!"

from this body!

we arrive in the shape of investigators to the final rooms

Deciders have at day's end to explore these matters
in contractual machinations
and death-to-the-poem corporate styles

and become inseparable from them

women called into the room
in a power arrangement where they stand before a Decider
    decidedly at disadvantage
feng shui decidely off for the women

eyes roam around the room, an array of Deciders behind desks
without much on them like prefab newscasters

and shiny surfaces like fortresses, reflections of Deciders' features
coming up at the women

one Decider at a desk before a woman raw and exposed

another flanked on the left with a trophy of counting coup

invoking regulations in a weak and whimpering monotone
"it's the rule"

patriarchs demand your silence where monosyllables stress
the company out

squint in light
glare seeping in from between slats of the blinds

By the shape of false governance came this shape of looking

The low-level Deciders were frantic when they heard of the escape of
Original Anne. A seventh-level Decider was caught in the dilemma
and wouldn't admit his weakness. The message from above was *never
admit a mistake, never be accountable.*

You had to keep decisions blamed on the lower-level Deciders. They
were not quite ready to handle the cinematic world the world of

reflections and double mirrors a fallen world might sputter off its reel
and die.
But this was metaphor.
There were scant reels in the New Deciding-Way.
Had not Chief Decider created a hell realm for prisoners?
Had he not voted to close the progressive library where thoughts of
freedom festered?
Libraries that might breed archivists?

He was swiftly demoted in the "new accountability."

"And now the tapes gone missing!"

"They're in the business of hell-on-earth, madrassas for anarchy"

heard how a poet gathered the fragments, wrote and
rewrote . . . erased

started again . . . little woman upstart

because when you write out a line with your body—structure it—
move it—
it gets free

that is what I wanted to see . . . how atom by atom your sentences
replicate beyond one another

I, poet, wanted a shape of her as a free agent before she dissolved
I wanted to catch her, un-canceled

And to let her know she could be missed
Even if I harbored dark thoughts toward her,
dark lady of my shadowy DNA
for she was the antiheroine of this tale

this is what happens when my singularities are alone
they want us to express their selves in triplicate
and steal or mingle among one another's texts, and double helixes

and appropriate and glorify themselves in the texts of others

but we see them and they are glad of that, enjoying exposure

the imprints they make in what are deceptively empty chambers but
none truly empty of ghosts, spirits, sense impressions

they come in mind trailing on willowy gossamer

sample: cartilaginous

sample: backbone

what they were on about . . . that they could plunge or fall in language

whose job it was to classify

but if you study smaller ones and their textures you may appreciate
the balk of similarity

loneliness of classifying others in an outcome of the study of
duplications
loneliness of erotics, may any two primates be truly alike?

but she is steady and outside time, ennobling it

and roots to be a scientist of illusion as she copies the originals

when you consider value of a shape of a form a genome barks *me too*
me too

which is plural and suggests a way to behave with accoutrements
that are symbolic, the skins of these trembling lines

classifying items of possession, of poem-objects, exquisite corpses,
and the jangling aces and pentacles, and voices that speak into ma-
chines

if she may consider her relation to the formerly alive parts of
formerly alive poems she will cheer up and be formally alive

she might stroke what is lonely and cold and listen to disembodied
voices
might push further into a void of identity

angels and savants fly in and out
messing with your Decider Radar

that they would be concentrated as well on the same kind of
machinations
or inventory or tone, but for darker control

countenance of an artist rising above others in her public cause

we might think of study . . . anecdote . . . fantasy a scenario
duplicity as of original poet mind to save it
we might think of stealing into a heart

crisp and figural is a description

in so many insomniacs
that fixes the face

we faces have use
when we can't sleep

it's like a wax museum in here
Heart of Archive, or storage units of rogue plutonium
as public pressure closes the bomb factory down

peering-in faces the archons take charge
to face an event of poetry enacted
before a crowd of suppliants facing arrest

rewind, we must hear that dulcet tune again. . . .
mega mega mega death-bomb enlighten

ideas in the event with masks
allowing of beauty and insomnia on a rocky divide

that was a title for something because I also have beautiful thoughts
when I can't sleep—
you too, as I say this facing you

these were the ideas of a nuclear-free zone
had in the event of facing off with police and other authorities
in the sure information a face would give beauty back to the world

as *tundra* derives from a word for "treeless"

up there to feel this business of lack of shadow, of tall things

"without trees" or "above the tree line" . . . an amphitheater of
summoning objects
or these living things back to themselves
come back! come back!
of struggling outside
and limitless, as of space

Archive hidden on a tundra, who would suspect?
one of the most uninhabitable places in the world

are you less grounded without a tree that's to consider and if you
are, why, how cruel yourselves often seem to trees in the rugged
landscape. Not cruel, negligent. Are you fighting for them in all the
ways they are captured and slaughtered?

seeing them, yes, but understanding?
not mistaken in all the selves you face daily, in the
face you face daily, and living with complex self that is a face-off

who speaks underneath your skin,
for fragile life-forms
that become institutionalized . . . or not
A map working its way through a body

Survival cartography

Chasm Falls: Original Anne half felt the jagged water drops

East Desolation Peak: Original Anne fell to her knees

Build the vault inside the Tundra, and she did,
hands clawing the hard inhospitable ground

green lipstick of a Heian mentor

back up, flash back

she who tamed the tiger
on a climb to the monastery
shook the demons out of her hair
lustrous
long as my doppelgänger shadow

long

as long a walk a long long way up here

New Deciders were organizing another war on a comparable Utopia

demolishing stacks in a library of powerful gnosis
tomes to guide and replenish imagination

artists would climb out of their foxholes
rounded up, exposed, and demand conservation
the ploy was "space," like nuclear power
who has the most capacity to make money off "space"?
nothing new, destroying books
a rogue state of small import had become refuge
pragmatic leaders were nervous: where to put our money down?
Deciders had Fear but saw Opportunity
were things looking up in the Deciding-Way?
you could be unabashed
Decider of what you might want to destroy
ask it of other Deciders and they surely rally
the weather was changing and New Deciders seemed happy
they would welcome the Drenchers and Wasters and Arsonists

they frolicked in their charnel ground of more deciding

but poetry was being planted in soil kept by women in robes of sleep
and utopic dream

Escaped and what she observed: What you are having here and must be careful not to step upon is fragile in so very delicate ground-obeying and earth-preserving forms and very most very sisterly soils. You might see dwarf shrubs or rosettes or mat or cushion plants. Very sisterly sounding and receptive if you are considering something about a guardian female. And gossamer the delicacy of life here, fragile endangered dwarfed. Here you have long long and cold winters and strong and very strong driving systirly winds. And very sestraly thoughts abound and even snow would help as an insulating swistarly layer for those plant and animal realms that seem to want to live here. We could try it being sororial as it is a place where a thin membrane exists between living and dying, and to go on living—if you could— you would be useful and sweostorly—if it wasn't prohibitive—you would be seeing that this form that is delicate even wordless but not antisocial and even raging to live—and like a newborn—seems to be struggling very hard.

could Archive be dwarfed, Original Anne mused

like the creatures of Tundra who struggle, becoming miniscule

could it be condensed?

condensare,

    the Poet admonished,
  look to the little ones

slaughtered, saying of something so small being slaughtered not so
   reckless as a couple of humans

humans standing reckless or contained

how to present thought and actions and deeds and words of the humans
   our Troubled Time

maybe not so close but vulnerable because they speak in silent
   walking

those who are troubled, those who bend

six weeks to grow to live to continue, delicate life forms hide under
   our speech holding them

someone walks someone exits someone escapes the rule of others

someone leaves you mustn't follow

rosette or mat plants or cushion plants underfoot be careful

the landscape reels back and forth stop a moment and capture an
   image of a youthful guardian

how now in dotage furrows worrying the future desecrations of poetry

veins bulge in anxiety of survival

shoe boxes of tape ready for transplant

ungrounded voices rising out of the floodplains of Samsara

afloat in New Weathers

long winters and cold and driving winds and

unpredictable weather fires and floods of Troubled Time

thin membrane between death or life or life in death

my sisters, you better know

Original Anne had repossession as she reentered the factious world
Original Anne had proprioception's stealth and glide
Original Anne might now reclaim all the receipts for the years
    she was possessed and on margin
her papers were in order
she could prove identity
she had been exonerated for the symbolic murders of Deciders
    who were exposed in public sessions of confession and shame

Deciders of low rank and lesser culpability were thrilled with the
    humiliation of the higher-rank Deciders

Poetry piped into their cells night and day

"Not us! Not us! It was those other Deciders did it" (they claimed now in
cage, many of them sick lying there in cage, weak in their Deciding-Way)

not as guilty being less exposed, they were under orders
    to revile poetry but did they really
when they ransacked the Quonset hut on the tundra they found
    nothing to connect Deciding with Poetry
yet sublime orality would hamper them forever in their Deciding-Way
    and for the exposure of Impostors

Original Anne drove stakes through the hearts of Impostors
their disguises had dissolved, wigs came tumbling off
makeup ran with the torrent created by strong waterfalls
they held their last meeting at the trial that was called to hear the
    crimes of the Deciders
decisions now often went in favor of the whims and egos of the
    Deciders, they got off too easy
and more importantly the wealth of the Deciders

who decided on ways to extract more power from the inner
   sanctums of planet earth
who would exhaust the resources of planet earth and exploit the
   New Weathers
and more disturbingly (and this showed their hand, *that they were*
   clearly insane) the strange perversions of the Deciders
who wanted to make decisions for all mankind about love
about who may or may not love another
who may or may not touch another, experience ecstasy with one
   another
who wanted to define rules for the care and control of all bodies
who would blame extreme weather patterns on lack of control of bodies
hurricane, tsunami, flood, tornado
"they have no control of their bodies"
"they love one another"
"cosmos out of joint"
"let them not love one another in this terrible way"
"it is not the Deciding-Way"
Original Anne stormed in and demanded retrieval of her memory
   stream
she charged in and reclaimed the essence of Archive
she had wrested Archive from the master-plan of the Deciders
she would not close her visions to the difficulties in North Africa
she would keep on the study of language and culture
but she had to let go of anything that did not tally with political reality
   "on the ground"
she did not compromise her involvement with crimes of terror and
   radical religious fervor
her name and the names of the subversive classes she taught were
   removed from the lists of the lackeys of the Deciders
she felt keenly the disinheritance of her institution which appeared now
   as a russet castle inhabited by enemies of poetry and imagination
   inhabited by the pervertors of the teaching, con artists who

preyed on the ignorance of tender supplicants
she had distance and she kept her distance in the hallways of
    archiveless night
the castle evaporated or rather disappeared from one world system
"it's all an illusion", said Decider Vishnu
while drones with their manic evaporating sounds of danger and
violence retreated into the distance, the little child deaf to the mach-
inations of power but feeling the vibrations
of a lighter time a future time

Archive buried in the frozen tundra, a treasure to last a thousand years
intonations of poets and of their fragile impermanence . . .

pity the New Deciders, she said
they will not inherit this earth
leave that to the slime molds, the protists,
those who inhabit the power of symbiosis
pity the Deciders pity their obsessions
pity their sick fixation with gender control
pity the lovers and mistresses of Kaneie and Genji

Deciders who frolic about the Shinden-zukuri mansion

while the women write of them
in subdued yet passionate tones

rain on tiled roofs
women rarely venturing beyond the veranda
receiving gentlemen callers from behind curtains
in their giant heaps of clothes. . . .

hiding a diary under a pillow stained with tears

Archive is not a portfolio.

This is my poem for now and future lovers, scrolled in my pillow book at dawn:

Start from a murmur of persons and rise up not like a veil of unsanctified tears; a work in love is never unsanctified enigma if not but pure flow and consent or rip in the veil which is sanctuary for persons be they same or other. As a waterfall never falling in the same sanctuary twice. An abode for our bodies, of union, of persons stepping up to the altar of ancestors together who were union who were civil who were convivial behind a veil. Step up, step it up, convivial. Show them, and rip the veil off the eyes of the enemies of veil. See it another way. Declare the space to be an abode of bodies. See through the waterfall to those behind a veil that was protecting the face of other, same-face same-base same-trace same-pace same-grace same-lace marriage. A civil veil. Or it is my vow my vowels and vocables to be this same which is never that same one in gender-constructed eros. Eros-faced marriage. We are never the same in same-sexed love. But law is civil and protects the abode of bodies. A body abode, a body abides. Say it: law is civil or rival is civet is civilized is civilians is not chilling. Gone is the time of boundaries of veils or tears of borderlines of separating cascades of enigmas and hiddenness. Gone is that chilling time that does not witness the desire to be seen to be witness of this union. Beyond a boundary "same" or "reciprocal" or "solidarity pacts." It is over, gone and done with, that violent time violent divide. Over, of hiding the shape of a bed, the shape of a clearing in a forest where you lie down, soft and mossy spot, and you might come together there, the ancient dark green moss and secluded spot you come to, again. Same and same and not same and sane. Decide our own bodies. You of former hiddenness and sorrow and lie down and come together and making do in the secret chamber sought that place you walked there you found a secluded spot below the Tundra where deer bedded down where deer waited and you stepped there and sank there on knees in a very hot devoted love where you rip the veils from the fear of prying eyes and welcome the presence of a natural world. And say something like "as sky is my witness . . . " "as earth is my witness . . . " Come here my weeds and remove these weeds to our sameness. See our sameness. And remove the borders to our sameness, "as weeds are my witness . . . " Come my hands to your natural weeds and remove the fear of our sameness and see the beauty of our sameness and not sameness. Touch the gossamer body of our sameness that you know, and hiddenness you know. Intangible. Clothing that waits by the side of bedding down and eyes you know in hiddenness. Fields of eyes not prying not hidden. It was natural and very natural to do this to be this to bed down in a clearing away from prying eyes and metabolic strangulation who said unnatural this contract a vow against perpetual wiring of denial. "as wilderness is my witness" "as wildness is my witness . . . " Take the vow in the wilderness. It is over, it is gone and done. It is over and done with being behind the shadow cloth of the marriage veil, behind it a valance, a balance, and what is the essence of this poetry as in music which knows no boundary. Rip the boundary that is veil. Where it tunes to the body of beautiful sameness but never the same music. Consciousness as in music and civil it is civil and civil it is a demand to be civil. As a cascade is civil, as from the tilling of fields and this world is a cultivation of new things in civility it is a sure thing to witness.

She put her dictum on the validity of love in all directions and buried it in a corner of the tundra:

詩に安全な世界を守ろう

KEEP THE WORLD SAFE FOR POETRY

काव्यायजगत्प्रशमनं भवतु

للشِعر آمِناً العَالم أبـق

for a joining that is not easy but is a joining work in love

Dream of duality in the phenomenal universe

veil of maya, a memory of rescue

illusion's dream

a false dichotomy?

MA = not

YA = that

I'll tear it off, pierce it

rend the veil from the other face

A gossamer web but not a trampoline
that will bounce out a Spider Woman's prey

Not a rubber band

Another word for strain-energy storage
might be resilience

A virtue of the movers and shakers of this shimmering world

Thinnest strains so they cannot be seen

UV-colored to lure; great train-energy storage;
efficient protein manufacture

Gossamer with binds to the more rigid:

branches, walls, twigs, grass stems,
the edges of roofs

all architectural structure

Lycosid spiderlings in a velocity gradient
of breeze and currents

There is the lift of gossamer
and the glide

The scramble of spiderlings
to the highest point
for a better launch

The drag-to-lift ratio

enough drag to engage the breeze

enough thin delicate strands to glide
and not parachute too soon

Gossamer mostly as seen floating in air

Archive, Archeion, Archon

See Jacques Derrida, *Archive Fever: A Freudian Impression* (University of Chicago Press, 1996).

I know this from Derrida, as written in the poem.

Archive Fever is a salient text, useful in a meditation on the overreaching *arkhe*, naming commencement and commandment as nomological principles. The contradiction, as Derrida explicates it, is the irony of an archive that shelters itself from this memory of *arkhe*, and also forgets it. We grow fainter in our memory and for the purpose of memory (versus erasure) require residence and command for our archives, and for a particular kind of concealment. Archeion is the domicile, which moves from private to public. Archons are those who command, who guard the documents. Poetry is by nature self-secret, but it is also fragile as document, and when recorded falls even more victim to decay and the unknowable technology of future guardians, if there be such. And who will be present to establish "voice recognition"?

Argana Café, Marrakech

Parts of this poem were written while traveling in North Africa, living and working for several weeks in Marrakech on two occasions. I first arrived shortly after the bombing of the Argana café in the medina of Jamaa el Fna, a terrorist act that killed seventeen people and wounded twenty-five on April 28, 2011. I also was working with a foundation that had a library and a center for translation, Dar Al-Ma'mûm (House of Wisdom), near Marrakech, named for the son of a caliph in Abbasid-era Iraq, and the notion of preservation was keen on people's minds, given the ransacking of museums and other sites of archive during frequent times of strife and war and inclement weather.

Caddis fly catch-nets

The name of the order of insects, *Trichoptera*, to which caddis flies belong, comes from the Greek words meaning "hair" and "wing." They are also called rail-flies or sedge-flies and resemble moths. The combination of hair and wing and a gossamer-like membranous quality—brought to my attention by Peter Warshall—was an eidolon for the poem.

Dark Lady of my DNA

Rosalind Franklin was a chemist whose research was used without her permission by Francis Crick and James Watson in their scientific breakthrough around DNA and the double helix.

demolishing stacks in a library

A reference to the much-debated renovation plan that would demolish seven floors of "stacks" at the New York Public Library. Many of the books would be stored under Bryant Park; with a new compromise generated by great protest from artists and writers and scholars, a new facility for storage would be built under the library. Many opponents have feared that the Central Library Plan will turn the historic Forty-Second Street Library into a giant Internet café.

Djinn: Jinn

Jinn (Arabic: جن *ǧinn*, singular جنّي *ǧinnī*; variant spelling *djinn*), or genies, are described in the Qur'an and in Arab folklore and Islamic mythology as occupying an alternative world to that of mankind. Jinn, humans, and angels make up the three sentient creations of Allah. The Qur'an mentions that jinn are made of smokeless flame or "scorching fire." Like human beings, the jinn may also be good, evil, or neutrally benevolent.

Djuna Barnes

I observed the celebrated and somewhat reclusive author of *Nightwood* in my Greenwich Village neighborhood as a child. Barnes stands in as a guardian here, and the site where she lived, at 5 Patchin Place, is an historic landmark. She reappears in New York City dreams. There is no visible plaque or marker at this site acknowledging her former residence there.

Holy Grail as a blank check

David Graeber's provocative idea of the Holy Grail as a blank check is from his book *DEBT: The First 5,000 Years* (Melville House, 2011), an inspirational tome for the Occupy movement.

". . . (I swear it) from the breath"

From Charles Olson, "Projective Verse," 1950.

Juan Goytisolo

Born January 6, 1936, in Barcelona, Juan Goytisolo is a Spanish poet, essayist, and novelist who has been living in voluntary self-exile in Marrakech. He has been largely responsible for the saving and preservation of the Jamaa el Fna square and market in Marrakech's medina, one of the Masterpieces of the Oral and Intangible Heritage of Humanity.

> [L]ike a spider, like an octopus, like a centipede slithering away, wriggling and writhing, escaping one's embrace, forbidding possession, there is no way of getting a firm grasp on it. . . .

> The spectacle of Jamaa el Fna is repeated daily and each day it is different. Everything changes—voices, sounds, gestures, the public which sees, listens, smells, tastes, touches. The oral tradition is framed by one much vaster—that we can call intangible. The Square, as a physical space, shelters a rich oral and intangible tradition.

> —Juan Goytisolo, on the active culture of Jamaa el Fna,
> Opening Meetings, May 15, 2001

one of two

> Ida used to sit and as she sat she said am I one or am I two. Little by little she was one of two, that is to say sometimes she went out as one and sometimes she went out as the other.

> —Gertrude Stein, *Ida* (Yale University Press, 2012)

moisopholon domos

House where one cultivates the muses. The myth survives that Sappho (approx. 630–570 BCE) was the headmistress of an academy or school of girls, akin to the Spartan *agelai* or *thiasos*, a sacred band.

the movies I appear in

The Edge, by Robert Kramer, 1968.
Brand X, by Wynn Chamberlain, 1970.
Renaldo and Clara, by Bob Dylan, 1978.

This section of the poem plays with the author's presumed resemblance to the actor Charlotte Rampling.

Narada and myths of doubles

See Wendy Doniger, *Dreams, Illusion, and Other Realities* (University of Chicago Press, 1984). Her study includes variants on the story of the Hindu sage Narada, who was transformed into a woman:

> The outer dream is a myth, which nourishes our hope that it is possible to break out of this prison of our secret loneliness to dream one another's dream.

seed vault

The Svalbard Global Seed Vault resides on the Norwegian island of Spitsbergen, a remote archipelago only eight hundred miles from the North Pole, a sanctuary providing refuge for seeds in case of a large-scale global crisis. They are held in trust for future survival.

Spider Woman

Creator deity for several indigenous U.S. tribes, including the Navajo, Keresan, and Hopi. Extraordinary weaver of life and the subject of many myths.

Spiderlings

Young spiders whose silk is sometimes referred to as gossamer.

storage units of rogue plutonium

A reference to Rocky Flats (1952–1992), a former nuclear weapons plant near Denver and Boulder, Colorado, that created plutonium-laced "triggers" for warheads. Although the structure has completely vanished, the soil continues to be toxic and hazardous, containing leaked amounts of plutonium, the half-life of which is close to a quarter of a million years. Many local citizens, including poets from the Jack Kerouac School of Disembodied Poetics community at Naropa University, as well as high-profile antinuclear activist Daniel Ellsberg, protested the site for two decades, facing harassment and arrest.

Temporary Autonomous Zone

See Hakim Bey, *T.A.Z.: The Temporary Autonomous Zone, Ontological Anarchy, Poetic Terrorism*, published by Autonomedia in New York City in 1991 with an anticopyright notice. The thinking in this book, essentially a manifesto, has influenced many cultural interventions and projects I've been personally involved with over the last decades. *T.A.Z.* investigates space that eludes formal structures of control.

Tirta Gangga

A water palace built by the Raga of Karangasem in eastern Bali, Indonesia. It has a spiritual connection to the river Ganges in India, and I cast a few of Allen Ginsberg's ashes into its pools, as a tribute to Allen's spiritual connection to India and to that river where he once bathed.

Tundra

From the Finnish word *tunturi*, meaning "treeless." Frost-molded landscapes, extremely low temperatures, low precipitation, poor nutrients, and a short growing season. A metaphor in this allegory for refuge.

Peter Warshall, ecobiologist

Where the conversation that became this book began, with "gossamer," "doppelgänger," and "archive" in the symbiosis of the "braided river."

> The fungal mat actually connects those trees, and what you have is not the image of all the Abrahamic religions, that things come out as the tree of life, with branches that go further and further apart with humans over here and elephants and frogs over there, but you actually have the image that symbiosis teaches, that life is a braided river. That things come

apart, like an algae and a fungus, and then come back together again. And then they spread out and come back together again. So the whole imagery of symbiosis is contrary to the prevailing religions all over the world in not thinking of life as a tree but more or less as a braided river.

—Peter Warshall, "Symbiosis," from *Civil Disobediences: Poetics and Politics in Action* (Anne Waldman and Lisa Birman, eds.; Coffee House Press, 2004)

women in robes of sleep and utopic dream

Joanna Macy, an ecophilosopher and activist, has advocated the concept of "nuclear guardianship," where citizens would train for this role and guard contaminated sites well into the future. She at one point imagined a ritual period of service here, a way "archons" might help preserve and honor a more sacred site, dressed in ceremonial uniforms or monks' robes. Some of these ideas become conflated in the poem, moving between thoughts of preservation, what's hidden or concealed, and what needs guardianship, as with both poetry and deadly nuclear waste.

Women's Poetry (male fantasies about women)

[I]t was men who determined the themes that were allowed in women's poetry. They decided what types of poetry to preserve; what types of poetry they would write in the voices of women, thereby setting the parameters within which women could write; and what types of poetry were expected of concubines and courtesans (who were obliged to write such poetry out of economic necessity). Such poetry tends to emphasize certain male fantasies about women, centered on the woman as longing for an absent lover. It seems clear that independent-minded women must have written outside the limitations imposed by male expectations, but precious little of that work has survived.

—David Hinton, "Women's Poetry in Ancient China," from *Classical Chinese Poetry: An Anthology* (Farrar, Strauss and Giroux, 2008)

A classic case of Decider mentality.

AUDIO LINES OF POETRY

Lines 11–19 on page 88, lines 2, 6–7, 19 on page 89, lines 1–2 on page 90, line 9 on page 91, line 9 on page 92, from the Naropa University Audio Archive Collection. All these lines are spoken/read by the poets themselves and have been transcribed from the tapes. Discrepancies might occur in printed versions of the poems.

"a sweeping revision" and "embers of the rain" from "Unctuous Platitudes," by John Ashbery

"the judge was the wind let the old things take over" from "Son of the Petrarch," by John Ashbery

"Truancy of will where she let it fall," "Door unlocked after the wounding," and "Thinking is not worrying" from "Lily," by Barbara Guest

"I made this book of sonnets" and "I, an island, sail" from *The Sonnets*, by Ted Berrigan

"I'm so in love with art that it will get me into the next world" from "It Springs on You," by Robin Blaser

"First, there were the FIRST PEOPLE" and "where human feet can squish the living daylights out of cowering anemone" from "In Memoriam," by Joanne Kyger

"I met Death—he was a sportsman" from "Cole's Island," Charles Olson

"the beauties of the Levant when we had them" and "not all the works of Mozart worth one human life" from *Revolutionary Letters*, by Diane di Prima

"a place so hip even the rats doing the hustle" and "think of what needs to be what needs to be" from "Afro-American Lyric," by Amiri Baraka

"in this wilderness of stone" from "Blues Variations," by Lorenzo Thomas

For further listening, access Archive.org and scroll down to "Naropa," or access the generous PennSound web site and portal.

Kai Silbley

Anne Waldman is the author of more than forty books including the seminal *Fast Speaking Woman*, published by City Lights in 1975, and has concentrated on the long poem as a cultural intervention with such projects as *Marriage: A Sentence*, *Structure of the World Compared to a Bubble*, and *Manatee/Humanity* (all three books published by Penguin Poets), as well as the antiwar feminist epic *The Iovis Trilogy: Colors in the Mechanism of Concealment*, published by Coffee House Press, and winner of the 2012 PEN Center USA Award for Poetry. She has been associated with the innovative wings of the Beat, Black Mountain, and New York School literary movements. She brings a remarkable intensity of her own into highly original "modal structures" of language and montage both written and performed. Deemed a "countercultural giant" by *Publishers Weekly*, Anne Waldman is also a performer, professor, editor, librettist, and cultural activist. Her numerous anthologies include *Nice To See You: Homage to Ted Berrigan*, *The Beat Book*, and the coedited collections *The Angel Hair Anthology*, *Civil Disobediences: Poetics and Politics in Action*, and *Beats at Naropa*. She has also collaborated with a number of visual artists, including Joe Brainard, Elizabeth Murray, George Schneeman, Richard Tuttle, Donna Dennis, Noah Saterstrom, and Pat Steir, as well as dancer/choreographer Douglas Dunn, musicians Steven Taylor and Ambrose Bye, writer/movie director Ed Bowes, and theater director Judith Malina. Her play *Red Noir* was produced by the Living Theatre in New York City in 2010. She is a cofounder with Allen Ginsberg of the Jack Kerouac School of Disembodied Poetics MFA program, and the artistic director of its Summer Writing Program at Naropa University, the first Buddhist-inspired school in the West. She has traveled for the U.S. State Department lecturing at Muslim colleges in Kerala, and she worked with schoolchildren in Marrakech, Morocco, in the spring of 2011 and 2012. Waldman is a recipient of the Poetry Society of America's Shelley Memorial Award, and is a Chancellor of the Academy of American Poets. Her extensive historical literary, art, and audio/video archive resides at the Hatcher Graduate Library in Ann Arbor, Michigan. See also fastspeakingmusic.com and the official web site www.annewaldman.org.

Penguin Poets

JOHN ASHBERY
Selected Poems
Self-Portrait in a Convex
  Mirror

TED BERRIGAN
The Sonnets

LAUREN BERRY
The Lifting Dress

JOE BONOMO
Installations

PHILIP BOOTH
Selves

JULIANNE BUCHSBAUM
The Apothecary's Heir

JIM CARROLL
Fear of Dreaming:
  The Selected Poems
Living at the Movies
Void of Course

ALISON HAWTHORNE DEMING
Genius Loci
Rope

CARL DENNIS
Callings
New and Selected
  Poems 1974–2004
Practical Gods
Ranking the Wishes
Unknown Friends

DIANE DI PRIMA
Loba

STUART DISCHELL
Backwards Days
Dig Safe

STEPHEN DOBYNS
Velocities: New and Selected
  Poems, 1966–1992

EDWARD DORN
Way More West: New and
  Selected Poems

ROGER FANNING
The Middle Ages

ADAM FOULDS
The Broken Word

CARRIE FOUNTAIN
Burn Lake

AMY GERSTLER
Crown of Weeds: Poems
Dearest Creature
Ghost Girl
Medicine
Nerve Storm

EUGENE GLORIA
Drivers at the Short-Time Motel
Hoodlum Birds
My Favorite Warlord

DEBORA GREGER
By Herself
Desert Fathers, Uranium
  Daughters
God
Men, Women, and Ghosts
Western Art

TERRANCE HAYES
Hip Logic
Lighthead
Wind in a Box

ROBERT HUNTER
Sentinel and Other Poems

MARY KARR
Viper Rum

WILLIAM KECKLER
Sanskrit of the Body

JACK KEROUAC
Book of Sketches
Book of Blues
Book of Haikus

JOANNA KLINK
Circadian
Raptus

JOANNE KYGER
As Ever: Selected Poems

ANN LAUTERBACH
Hum
If in Time: Selected Poems,
  1975–2000
On a Stair
Or to Begin Again

CORINNE LEE
PYX

PHILLIS LEVIN
May Day
Mercury

WILLIAM LOGAN
Macbeth in Venice
Madame X
Strange Flesh
The Whispering Gallery

ADRIAN MATEJKA
Mixology

MICHAEL MCCLURE
Huge Dreams: San Francisco
  and Beat Poems

DAVID MELTZER
David's Copy: The Selected
  Poems of David Meltzer

ROBERT MORGAN
Terroir

CAROL MUSKE-DUKES
An Octave above Thunder
Red Trousseau
Twin Cities

ALICE NOTLEY
Culture of One
The Descent of Alette
Disobedience
In the Pines
Mysteries of Small Houses

LAWRENCE RAAB
The History of Forgetting
Visible Signs: New and Selected
  Poems

BARBARA RAS
The Last Skin
One Hidden Stuff

MICHAEL ROBBINS
Alien vs. Predator

PATTIANN ROGERS
Generations
Wayfare

WILLIAM STOBB
Absentia
Nervous Systems

TRYFON TOLIDES
An Almost Pure Empty Walking

ANNE WALDMAN
Gossamurmur
Kill or Cure
Manatee/Humanity
Structure of the World
  Compared to a Bubble

JAMES WELCH
Riding the Earthboy 40

PHILIP WHALEN
Overtime: Selected Poems

ROBERT WRIGLEY
Anatomy of Melancholy and Other
  Poems
Beautiful Country
Earthly Meditations: New and
  Selected Poems
Lives of the Animals
Reign of Snakes

MARK YAKICH
The Importance of Peeling
  Potatoes in Ukraine
Unrelated Individuals Forming a
  Group Waiting to Cross

JOHN YAU
Borrowed Love Poems
Paradiso Diaspora